BAP Developers: A Guide to Mobile and Desktop Application

·2219-5
2220-1

ISBN-13 (electronic): 978-1-4842-2220-1

...trol Number: 2017946310

...ehan Zaidi

...ver image designed by Freepik

Managing Director: Welmoed Spahr
Editorial Director: Todd Green
Acquisitions Editor: Susan McDermott
Development Editor: Laura Berendson
Technical Reviewer: Diego Dora
Coordinating Editor: Rita Fernando
Copy Editor: Bill McManus

Distributed to the book trade worldwide by Springer Science+Business Media New York,
233 Spring Street, 6th Floor, New York, NY 10013. Phone 1-800-SPRINGER, fax (201) 348-4505, e-mail
orders-ny@springer-sbm.com, or visit www.springeronline.com. Apress Media, LLC is a California LLC
and the sole member (owner) is Springer Science + Business Media Finance Inc (SSBM Finance Inc).
SSBM Finance Inc is a **Delaware** corporation.

For information on translations, please e-mail rights@apress.com, or visit http://www.apress.com/
rights-permissions.

Apress titles may be purchased in bulk for academic, corporate, or promotional use. eBook versions and
licenses are also available for most titles. For more information, reference our Print and eBook Bulk Sales web
page at http://www.apress.com/bulk-sales.

Any source code or other supplementary material referenced by the author in this book is available to readers
on GitHub via the book's product page, located at www.apress.com/9781484222195. For more detailed
information, please visit http://www.apress.com/source-code.

Printed on acid-free paper

JavaScript
SAP ABAP D

A Guide to Mobile and Deskto
Development

▮▮▮

Rehan Zaidi

JavaScript Essentials for SAP A
Development

Rehan Zaidi
Karachi, Pakistan

ISBN-13 (pbk): 978-1-4842
DOI 10.1007/978-1-4842

Library of Congress Co

Copyright © 2017 by R

This work is subject t
material is concern
broadcasting, repr
and retrieval, ele
hereafter develo

Trademarked
every occurre
editorial fash

The use in
not identi
propriet

While
neith
omi
co

C

Apress®

I dedicate this book to my Mother

Contents at a Glance

Contents

About the Author

Rehan Zaidi is a consultant for several international SAP clients (both onsite and remotely) on a wide range of SAP technical and functional requirements, and also provides writing and documentation services for their SAP- and ABAP-related products. He started working with SAP in 1999 and writing about his experiences in 2001. Rehan has written several articles for both *SAP Professional Journal* and *HR Expert,* and also has a number of popular SAP- and ABAP-related books to his credit.

Rehan is co-founder of IMZ Technologies, which provides SAP consulting to companies and helps clients (both onsite and remotely) with their SAP technical requirements (ABAP, Workflow, Quick development of Fiori apps, and S/4 HANA-related requirements). Rehan also creates documentation and training manuals for a number of companies based in the United States.

Rehan has clients located in a number of countries and continents, including the Middle East (GCC region), North America, and Europe. He also is currently working on a new ERP programmer magazine.

Rehan may be contacted via email at rehan@imztechno.com and erpdomain@gmail.com.

About the Technical Reviewer

Diego Dora is the Managing Director of sovanta AG's labs in Buenos Aires, Argentina. He has over 15 years' experience in the IT industry wearing different hats, including Developer, Software Architect, Development Manager, and Project Manager. Throughout his career, Diego has focused on developing enterprise business applications for international companies. He has extensive experience in JavaScript, SAPUI5, SAP Systems, SAP ABAP, SAP Cloud Platform, SAP HANA, and SAP Fiori, among other SAP technologies. Currently he is researching the subject of machine learning in the modern enterprise.

Acknowledgments

I am very thankful to both of my parents, in particular my mother (my main source of motivation and strength in life), and all my friends and well-wishers for their best wishes and prayers.

I am grateful to Susan McDermott for providing me the opportunity to write another SAP-related book that will be published from the United States. Many thanks to Rita Fernando for all the help and guidance during the writing and editing process.

I am very grateful to Diego Dora for his technical edits. Despite his personal problems and difficulties, he helped us make this book ready for publishing.

And I am very indebted to all the people of Apress who have worked on the development of this book.

Introduction

Mobile and desktop application development for SAP Fiori is a very important and popular topic for SAP developers. It requires SAP development tools based in JavaScript (JS). A major problem faced by many members of the SAP ABAP community is that they have little to no knowledge of JS. This book addresses that problem. Written as a quick guide for SAP ABAP developers to easily master JavaScript, this book will equip you with the necessary skills to develop mobile and desktop applications.

The primary emphasis of this book is on the parts of the JS language that are useful from the perspective of an ABAP developer. The book starts with a brief introduction to HTML, the basics of JS, and how to create and run a simple JS program. It then dives into the details of the language, showing you how to make simple programs. Next, it covers in detail loops, mathematical operations, and string and regular expression in JS. The book then gives you a taste of functions, followed by objects and object-oriented programming in JavaScript. Code examples and screenshots are provided throughout the book to help you fully understand JS. Finally, this book includes a chapter on miscellaneous topics, including JS best practices and recommendations.

This book is intended for SAP professionals, ABAP users, and university students. A brief overview of the chapters follows:

Chapter 1: Introduction to JavaScript for ABAP. This chapter is an introduction to JavaScript for ABAP developers. It starts with the prerequisite knowledge for ABAP developers learning JavaScript. It next covers the basics of JavaScript, followed by the typical differences between the ABAP and JavaScript languages. Finally, it presents a very simple running JS program and shows you the necessary steps to create it yourself.

Chapter 2: Getting Your Feet Wet with JavaScript Language. This chapter first gives you an overview of the Window object. Next, it describes in detail the data types that JavaScript provides. Then, demo programs will show you how to display data to the user in a dialog box, debug your web page in a web browser console, and receive input from the user via a dialog box. The final section provides a list of reserved words in the JS language. This chapter provides the foundation of the JS language.

Chapter 3: Operators in JavaScript. As with all languages, the operators are very important for JS programmers and developers. This chapter starts with coverage of the arithmetic operators. Next, it introduces the comparison operators and logical operators that are used for formulating conditional checks in JS programs. Finally, the bitwise, assignment, and string operators are discussed.

Chapter 4: Control Structures in JavaScript. Once you have a good grasp of the operators in JS, you will be ready to see the control structures provided by JavaScript in action. This chapter first looks at compound statements and coding examples. It then discusses the if...else statements and switch statements that are used for formulating conditions in programs. The chapter next covers in detail the loops applicable in JavaScript, such as the for loop, for...in loop, while loop, and do...while loop. Plenty of demo examples are provided to enable you to strengthen your understanding of the control structures.

Chapter 5: Regular Expressions. JavaScript provides the option of solving problems using regular expressions, which help fulfill requirements in a small number of code lines. This chapter discusses the RegExp object needed for working with regular expressions in JavaScript. It also covers the method of searching for and replacing patterns within a text stream. Finally, it provides actual problems and coding in JS using regular expressions.

Chapter 6: Functions in JavaScript. Functions play an important role in JS. This chapter begins with an overview of functions in JavaScript and the advantages they provide. You will see the syntax required to create functions, along with a simple program containing a function definition. Separate sections will show you how to create a program that calls a function and how to create a function that calls another function. In addition, you will see typical coding examples and requirements met via functional programming.

Chapter 7: More on Functions. Because functions are a major topic, two chapters are devoted to their coverage. Building on the coverage of the basics in Chapter 6, this chapter focuses on the advanced topics within the functions landscape. First, you will see how to use functions as variables. Then, you will be introduced to the concept of self-executing functions. Next, you will learn about nested functions— functions within functions. The chapter closes, appropriately, with a discussion of the very useful "closure" concept.

Chapter 8: Objects in JavaScript and Programming. As with ABAP, JavaScript allows you to create objects. However, the concepts pertaining to object creation in the two languages are not the same. This chapter is dedicated to object creation, instantiation, and inheritance. It starts with a general overview of object-oriented programming before drilling down to objects in JS and their syntax. It introduces the `this` operator in detail, then covers the various ways of creating objects, followed by the instantiation steps using the `new` keyword. Once you have a basic understanding of objects, the chapter moves on to inheritance as implemented in JS using prototypes. The chapter contains real-life examples of objects and subobjects throughout, along with ample code listings demonstrating how to implement them in JavaScript.

Chapter 9: Other Useful Objects in JavaScript. By this point in the book, you will be familiar with quite a few built-in objects in JavaScript. This chapter introduces a number of other useful objects, such as `Array`, `Boolean`, `Date`, and `String`, and the methods they provide. You will see several programming examples that implement these methods.

Chapter 10: Working with JSON. This chapter covers the important topic of JavaScript Object Notation. To begin, you will be introduced to JSON and see some typical examples. You will then see how the JSON arrays and objects work in JS programs. The chapter then covers two important functions, `stringify` and `parse`, used for programming with JS. As in all chapters, ample programming examples will be provided.

Chapter 11: Miscellaneous Topics. Chapter 11 contains several JS topics that are very useful but do not fit well in any of the other chapters. It starts with an overview of strict mode and how it affects the syntax check. Next, it covers error handling in JavaScript. A separate section covers the typical errors that you should avoid while working with JS. The chapter then explains debugging and troubleshooting JS programs. Last but not least, best practices for JS programming and tips for performance improvement are provided.

CHAPTER 1

■ ■ ■

Introduction to JavaScript

This chapter serves an introduction to JavaScript for ABAP developers. We will start with the prerequisite knowledge for learning JavaScript. Then, we will cover the basics of JavaScript, followed by some of the differences between ABAP and JavaScript. Next, we will look at a very simple program and the necessary steps for you to create it yourself.

Brief JavaScript Background

JavaScript is a high-level, dynamic, untyped language standardized in the ECMAScript language specification. Together with Hypertext Markup Language (HTML) and Cascading Style Sheets (CSS), JavaScript is another important technology that originally powered the Web Applications Architecture. JavaScript (JS) is supported by all modern web browsers, and is used by the majority of websites and web applications today. In the beginning, typical examples for the use of JavaScript included creating interactive effects on web pages and conducting form data validations on websites. Since then, a number of libraries have been written in JS, such as jQuery.

■ **Note** There is a common misconception that JavaScript and Java are similar. They are unrelated and have different semantics. The syntax of JavaScript is derived from the C programming language.

Also, the JS language is used in server-side programming as a runtime engine for several different browser engines such as V8 (Google Chrome) and SpiderMonkey (Firefox). One of the most widely known and used JS runtime environments is called NodeJS.

JavaScript has some syntactical similarities with the C language such as the switch and if statements and the while and do while loops. In JavaScript, types are linked with values, rather than with variables. For example, a variable named myvar could be assigned a string first and subsequently rebound to a number.

JavaScript is a case-sensitive language, meaning any language keywords, variable names, and function names must be written with consistent capitalization. The keyword case, for example, must be written "case" and not "Case" or "CASE."

JavaScript is a *multiparadigm* language that allows imperative programming, object-oriented programming, and functional programming. It allows you to work with text, numbers, dates, and arrays. Regular expression processing capability is also provided in JavaScript. However, JS does not offer any networking or graphics features. JavaScript supports prototypes (in contrast to many other object-oriented languages, such as ABAP) that use classes for inheritance. Many class-based features may be programmed using prototypes in JavaScript.

© Rehan Zaidi 2017
R. Zaidi, *JavaScript Essentials for SAP ABAP Developers*, DOI 10.1007/978-1-4842-2220-1_1

Inside a JavaScript Program

This section introduces the various different code elements of a JavaScript program in detail.

A JavaScript program is composed of a number of statements. Each statement ends with a semicolon (;). JavaScript differentiates between an expression and a statement. A statement may be composed of literals, variables, and expressions. A given JS statement might span multiple lines. Also, it is possible for more than one statement to be written in a single line.

Comments form an important part of any code. They are disregarded by JavaScript, but they are an essential tool for programmers to document the purpose of their code for later review. There are two types of comments you can add to a JavaScript program. First, you can add a single-line comment as shown here:

```
var num = 1; // from here comments start
```

As you can see, single-line comments begin with a double slash (//). All subsequent code/text written on that line is treated as comment text. No ending punctuation is necessary to mark the end of a single-line comment; the end of the line serves that purpose.

JavaScript also allows you to specify multiline comments. These may be enclosed between /* and */, and may comprise one or more lines. Within multiline comments, nesting is not possible. Attempting to nest multiline comments will produce a syntax error. Listing 1-1 shows an example that is not acceptable in JS.

Listing 1-1. Incorrectly Nested Comments

```
/*  this is comment 1
/*  this is comment 2  */
*/
```

As you can see, this example attempts to nest comment 2 within comment 1, which is not allowed and will give a syntax error.

Within a JavaScript program, statements are executed line by line (i.e., sequentially). A set of statements may be grouped together to form a block. The start and end of a block are denoted by curly brackets ({ }). These blocks may include code within a function (functions are similar to subroutines in ABAP) or code within if statements or switch statements.

A JS program may include a number of literals. You use literals in JS to denote fixed values (in contrast to variables) to be used within your programs. Some examples of these literals are integers and string literals.

In JavaScript, string literals are enclosed within a set of double quotes ("") or a set of single quotes (''), whereas ABAP strings are enclosed within single quotes only. Some other types of literals are array literals, Boolean literals, and object literals.

Creating a Simple JS Program

Now that you have some basic knowledge of JavaScript, this section shows you how to make a simple program, and then explains the various parts of it.

You will create a small program that displays a message saying "My first JS Program" in a pop-up dialog box. There is a built-in function alert in JS that lets you display a message to the user. This function may take as input as either a number or string in the form of a literal or variable.

The code for this program is shown in Listing 1-2.

Listing 1-2. Program for Displaying Text in Pop-up Dialog Box

```html
<html>
   <body>
      <script>
            alert("First JS program by an ABAP Developer");
      </script>
   </body>
</html>
```

As you can see, the program uses a string literal (within double quotes) to display the message to the user. Running this example displays a message in a pop-up dialog box, as shown in Figure 1-1.

Figure 1-1. *Program output*

A Quick Look at HTML

JavaScript code cannot be executed on its own. It relies on the runtime environment to include/import scripts (e.g., HTML <script> elements). So, in order to program JavaScript, you need to know some HTML. A full discussion of HTML is beyond the scope of this book. This section introduces the basics of the HTML language and shows you the usage of an HTML tag and its corresponding browser output.

HTML is the language used to create web pages. Within the web page source code text, you have a number of tags. Simply defined, *tags* are codes in an HTML document that begin with the symbol < and end with >. Tags mostly appear in pairs, and a pair of tags instructs the browser how to treat the text appearing within the tag pair.

Each tag has a special meaning and has its own effect. The tags are read by the browser and interpreted accordingly. The tags are not displayed by the browser. The browser then renders and displays the web page to the viewer.

■ **Note** HTML is not a case-sensitive language: <html>, <HTML>, and <Html> all have the same effect. However, you must make sure that the end tag, such as </HTML>, contains a forward slash, not a backward slash. Writing <\HTML> will cause problems.

At this stage, you only need to know the details of HTML that will help you to run the JS code that you will write. A number of elements exist in an HTML document that are represented as tags:

- The HTML tags, <HTML> and </HTML>, mark the beginning and end of the HTML document. The browser renders the page based on the information contained within the HTML tags. Make sure that no code is written after the </HTML> tag, which marks the end of the HTML document. Within the HTML page, you have a <HEAD> and a <BODY> tag.

- The HEAD tags encompass the general information pertaining to the document, such as the usage of the page and linkage with other documents and resources. For example, a pair of tags may contain information about the JS file and CSS code relevant to the web page. Within the HEAD are the TITLE tags that are used to specify the title of the document. The title is displayed at the top of window of the browser. The TITLE tags also contain metadata about the document.

- <BODY> and </BODY> encompass information about the page body—the actual content rendered when the page is loaded by the browser. Some of the elements contained within this pair of tags are the header and footer. Within the body, you may display a number of text lines, tables, forms, and graphics. You may have a number of headings such as <heading1>, <heading2>, and so on. Using the <P> tag, you can also specify where a new paragraph starts. The browser reads the various elements within the body and renders the page accordingly.

Now you are prepared to look at how to write your first HTML code. A simple HTML program without any JavaScript in it is shown in Figure 1-2.

```
file:///C:/Users/rehanz/Desktop/Test.htm - Original Source         —  □  ×

File  Edit  Format
 1  <!DOCTYPE html>
 2  <html>
 3   <head>
 4     <title>My first Web Page</title>
 5   </head>
 6
 7  <body>
 8  <h1>This is level 1 Heading</h1>
 9   <p>This is a paragraph with text shown in <B> bold </b>.</p>
10
11   <p>This is another paragraph with text shown in <I> Italics </I>.</p>
12
13   <p>This is another paragraph with text shown as <U> Underlined </u>.</p>
14
15  </body>
16  </html>
```

Figure 1-2. *HTML code sans JavaScript*

The output of the code from Figure 1-2 is shown in Figure 1-3.

This is level 1 Heading

This is a paragraph with text shown in **bold** .

This is another paragraph with text shown in *Italics* .

This is another paragraph with text shown as <u>Underlined</u> .

Figure 1-3. *HTML code output*

If there is a syntax error in your HTML code, the browser still produces an output. However, you may not get the desired result. Consider, for example, the same code shown in Figure 1-2 with the </H1> tag in the body wrongly written as <\H1> (i.e., with a backslash). In this case, the entire set of text lines is displayed in the Heading style, as shown in Figure 1-4.

This is level 1 Heading<\h1>

This is a paragraph with text shown in bold .

This is another paragraph with text shown in *Italics* .

Figure 1-4. *Wrong output of HTML page*

Putting JavaScript in HTML Code

This section shows you how to add your JavaScript code from earlier in the chapter to the simple HTML page from the previous section. You can choose any of several approaches to do this. The simplest approaches are to write the entire JS code either in the head or the body of the HTML page. It is also possible to write the JS code as a separate file and include the name of the file in your HTML code. Let's consider these approaches one by one. Note that they all produce the same output in the browser display.

Writing JS Code Within the <HEAD> and </HEAD> Tags

The first approach is to include the entire JavaScript code within the HEAD element. For example, you can embed the JS code that you wrote in Listing 1-2 in the HTML code created in the previous section (shown in Figure 1-2). The HTML code containing the JavaScript is shown in Listing 1-3.

Listing 1-3. HTML Code with JS Code in HEAD

```
<!DOCTYPE html>
<html>
 <head>
   <title>My first Web Page</title>
    <script>
      alert("First JS program by an ABAP Developer");
    </script>
  </head>
<body>
</body>
</html>
```

As you can see, the single-line JS script is written within the HEAD tags. When the browser reaches the <script> tag, it executes the JS script. Once the script execution is complete, the browser returns to the HTML and executes the remaining HTML code after the </script> tag.

Writing JS Code Within the <BODY> and </BODY> Tags

Another approach is to include the JavaScript code within the BODY element, before the </BODY> tag (i.e., the end of the body), as shown in Listing 1-4. From the standpoint of the user, the effect will be the same.

Listing 1-4. Adding JavaScript in the HTML Body

```
<!DOCTYPE html>
<html>
 <head>
   <title>My first Web Page</title>
 </head>
<body>
<script>
     alert("First JS program by an ABAP Developer");
</script>
</body>
</html>
```

As with the previous approach, when the browser reaches the <script> tag, it executes the JS script, after the completion of which it returns to the HTML and executes the remaining HTML code after the </script> tag.

Creating JS Code in a Separate File

Another approach commonly used is to include the JS code in a file separate from the HTML code and include a link to the JS file within the HTML code. This approach offers a few advantages: it makes the HTML code and JavaScript code both easier to understand and maintain. Listing 1-5 shows how to link to a JS file within the HTML code.

■ **Note**   When linking an external JS file to HTML code, make sure that the name of the JS file is written in the correct case. For example, do not write Code.js as code.js or CODE.JS.

Listing 1-5. Addressing a JS File in HTML Code

```
<!DOCTYPE html>
<html>
 <head>
   <title>My first Web Page</title>
   <script src="Code.js">   // JS file name
   </script>
 </head>
<body>
</body>
</html>
```

This example assumes that the JavaScript code is contained in a separate file, in the same directory where the HTML code resides. As you can see, the name of the file that contains the JS code (in this case, Code.js) is specified within the HEAD element. You must make sure that you write the name of the file in the correct case.

Again, once the <script> tag is reached, the browser executes the JS script. After the script execution is complete, the browser returns to the HTML and executes the remaining HTML code after the </script> tag.

Variable Declaration in JavaScript

Variable declaration is an important part of any programming language. Declaring variables enables you to assign symbolic names to values that you use in your programs. A JavaScript variable name must start with one of the following:

- A letter (including uppercase characters *A* through *Z* and lowercase characters *a* through *z*)

- An underscore (_)

- A dollar sign ($)

The name cannot start with a digit (0-9), but subsequent characters may be digits. Some examples of allowed variable names are Nu_hits, Mytemp13, and _myname.

Variables defined in JavaScript are either *global*, with a global execution context, or *local*, specific to a particular function (we will discuss this in the later part of the book). A local variable is visible/accessible only within the function in which it is defined and not outside that function. Global variables are visible/accessible to the entire JS program.

Variables in JavaScript are declared using the var keyword. Here is the syntax:

```
var num;
```

It is also possible to declare a variable and initialize it in the same line of code:

```
var num = 1;
```

You may also link two variable declarations in a single line (chaining them together using a comma):

```
var num1, num2;
```

It is also possible to initialize either or both of the variables in a single line of code:

```
var num1, num2 = 1;
```

7

You do not need to specify the type of the variable. The declaration takes the type from the value that is assigned to it.

▪ **Note** In contrast to ABAP, JavaScript lets you declare variables and then change their type.

You may also use the same var statement to declare a variable and initialize it with a value, and then assign the variable with its value to another variable:

```
var num1 = 10;
var num2 = num1;
```

As you can see, variable num1 is declared and initialized with a value of 10. After the second statement, the num2 variable is declared as a number and is assigned the value 10. After the statements, both variables have the value 10.

It is also possible to change the type of the variable later. For example, if you have variable num1 as a number, you can later change it to a string, as shown in this example:

```
var num1 = 10;
num1 = "my string";
```

In JavaScript, you may also declare a variable after it has been used. In other words, you may use a variable even before its declaration. Consider the following short piece of code:

```
num1 =  10;
var num1;
```

In this case, we have a variable named num1 to which the value 10 is assigned. Later in the code is the definition of the variable using the var keyword. This feature of JS is known as *variable hoisting*. When a JS program is loaded and executed, all the var statements that declare variables are processed first (i.e., before the rest of the program code).

As mentioned earlier, JavaScript is a case-sensitive language. That means you can create variables with the same letters but in different cases. For example, consider the following example:

```
var message = "Second JS Program - Message 1";
var MESSAGE = "Second JS Program - Message 2";
```

This code defines two separate variables, message and MESSAGE, each of which is assigned a different string value. This practice is discouraged to avoid mix-ups.

Using Eclipse

There is no single editor for creating JavaScript programs. You have a number of options, such as

- Notepad
- SAP Web IDE
- Scratchpad
- Notepad++

In this section and throughout the book, I will demonstrate creating JavaScript programs using my editor of choice, Eclipse IDE. Showing you the entire Eclipse installation process is beyond the scope of this chapter. You should be able to install it fairly easily via the instructions available online at www.eclipse.org, where you can also download Eclipse.

Once you have successfully installed Eclipse, double-click the shortcut on your desktop, as shown in Figure 1-5.

Figure 1-5. *Eclipse shortcut*

■ **Note** All the examples and screenshots were tested in Windows.

Alternately, if you are using Windows, you may use the Programs menu to open Eclipse. Both options take you to the start screen of the Eclipse editor, as shown in Figure 1-6.

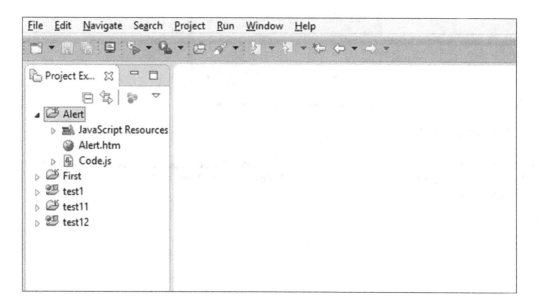

Figure 1-6. *Eclipse editor*

You now need to create an Eclipse JavaScript project. Choose the menu path File ➤ New ➤ Project. The New Project dialog box appears, as shown in Figure 1-7. Expand the JavaScript folder, select the JavaScript Project node, and click the Next button.

Figure 1-7. *Creating a JavaScript project*

On the wizard screen that appears, enter the name of the project (for purposes of this example, enter **First**). Do not change any other values on the screen and click the Finish button. The screen now appears as shown in Figure 1-8.

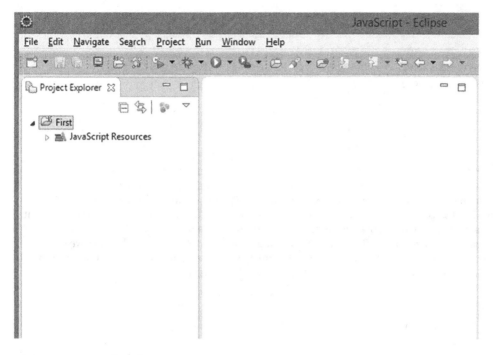

Figure 1-8. *Project "First"*

In the left panel, you can see that the project named First initially has no HTML or JavaScript files. You will now add both JavaScript and HTML files to this project. To add JavaScript code, simply right-click the First project node and choose New ➤ JavaScript Source File. In the dialog box that appears, enter the name of the file; for purposes of this example, enter **Code.js**. Then, click the Finish button.

The left pane will appear as shown in Figure 1-9.

Figure 1-9. *Code.js node added*

As you can see, a new Code.js node has been added to the First project folder. To add code to the Code.js file, simply double-click the node. The right pane changes as shown in Figure 1-10.

```
*Code.js ⌗
1      var message = "Second JS Program - Message 1";
2      var MESSAGE = "Second JS Program - Message 2";
3        alert(message);
4        alert(MESSAGE);
5
6
```

Figure 1-10. *JavaScript editor*

Simply add the code in the program as shown in Figure 1-10, and save the code using the key combination CTRL+S. As you can see, this example uses two variables that have similar names but different case (MESSAGE and message). It also uses two alert statements to output the values to the user.

Next, you need to add an HTML file to your project. Right-click the folder First and choose New ➤ File. In the dialog box that appears, enter a name for the file with an html extension (for this example, **First.html**). Enter the code of the html in the HTML editor in the right panel (see Figure 1-11).

```
First.htm ⌗
1  <!DOCTYPE html>
2⊖ <html>
3⊖   <head>
4       <title>My first Web Page</title>
5⊖      <script src="Code.js">
6       </script>
7     </head>
8⊖ <body>
9  </body>
10 </html>
```

Figure 1-11. *HTML editor*

As you can see, this example uses the <script> tag to address the Code.js file that you have made.

Next, save your project. You may now test your code within Eclipse. For this, right-click the HTML file node and choose Run ➤ Browser.

You will see the output in the right panel. Because you have written two alert statements in the program, the output of the first alert statement is displayed in a dialog box, as shown in Figure 1-12.

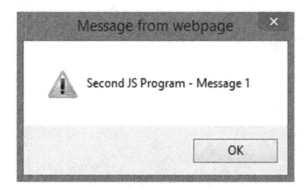

Figure 1-12. *JavaScript editor displaying an alert*

Clicking the OK button of the first dialog box will display the second dialog box.

You have successfully created a JavaScript program in Eclipse, giving you a foundation on which to build in subsequent chapters.

Summary

This opening chapter of the book covered the basics of JavaScript. You saw how to define and use variables in your programs, and how to make a simple JS program. In addition, you had a look at the Eclipse IDE for creation of JavaScript programs and HTML code. In the next chapter, you will explore the language in further detail, including the data types supported in the JavaScript language.

CHAPTER 2

A Step Ahead in JavaScript

Having learned the basics of JavaScript and the prerequisites for running a JavaScript (JS) program in Chapter 1, you are ready to move on to details of the JS language. This chapter first gives you an overview of the Window object. Next, it describes in detail the data types that JavaScript provides. Then, demo programs will show you how to display data to the user in a dialog box, debug your web page in the console of a web browser, and take input from the user via a dialog box. The final section of the chapter presents a list of reserved words of the JS language.

Window Object

One important concept within JavaScript is the Window object. The window object represents an open window within a browser. This section describes this object and the properties and methods that it provides.

Within a JS program, all variables declared outside of any function are global in nature. They remain alive during the entire execution of a web page. Global variables are properties of this object. The set of global variables is accessible via the global Window object. Any component of the window object is accessible by using dot notation (.).

To better understand the Window object, consider the following excerpt of a JS program:

```
var num1 = 10;
window.num1 = 20 ;
alert (num1);
```

This syntax declares a variable num1 and assigns to it the value 10. It then uses the window object to access num1 and assigns it the value 20. The short JS program outputs the value as shown in Figure 2-1.

Figure 2-1. *Program output*

© Rehan Zaidi 2017
R. Zaidi, *JavaScript Essentials for SAP ABAP Developers*, DOI 10.1007/978-1-4842-2220-1_2

As you can see, the value of 20 is displayed rather than 10. This is because the variable num1 resides within the global container accessed via the window object. When you assign the value 20, it refers to the same variable num1.

The Window object contains a number of properties and methods and is supported by all major browsers. Some of the important properties associated with it are listed and briefly described in Table 2-1.

Table 2-1. *Important Properties of the Window Object*

Property	Purpose
status	Sets or returns status bar text at bottom of browser
name	Sets or returns the name of the window
fullScreen	Indicates full-screen display of the window
innerHeight	Sets the height of the window content area, including the horizontal scrollbar
innerWidth	Sets the width of the window content area
length	Sets the number of frames in the window

In addition, the Window object has many useful methods. Some of the important methods are listed and briefly described in Table 2-2.

Table 2-2. *Important Methods of the Window Object*

Method	Purpose
alert()	Shows an alert box to user with message text and OK button
prompt()	Generates a dialog box for the user to enter input
print()	Writes the content of the window in question
open()	Creates a new window in the browser
close()	Closes a window
confirm()	Shows a dialog with OK and Cancel buttons with appropriate message
createPopup()	Creates a pop-up window (this method works in Internet Explorer)

These methods may be called in all parts of a JS program. While calling these methods, you may either use the Window object or call these methods without it. Consider the following example:

```
Window.alert("Hello"); //  incorrect, as Window must be written in lowercase i.e. window
window.alert(text);     //  correct
alert("Hello");         // correct
```

The preceding two statements have the same effect. It is not necessary to use the call along with the Window object.

■ **Note**   When calling the window object, always use lowercase letters.

Data Types in JavaScript

Chapter 1 briefly introduced the available data types in JS. This section explores the various data types supported in JavaScript in greater depth. In JavaScript, the variable is given the type that is assigned at a given instance.

Overall, there are six data types that exist in JavaScript, as summarized in Table 2-3. The following subsections describe them in more detail and show how to declare them.

Table 2-3. *Data Types and Their Purpose*

Name of Type	Purpose
string	A set of characters
number	Whole numbers, negative or positive, or number with various decimals
undefined	Variable having this type has been defined but without value
null	Intentional or explicit specification for a variable having no value
object	Set of properties and property values unordered
Boolean	Contains true or false

String

A string is a sequence of characters of various lengths. Typical examples include `"John123"` and `"John is a nice person"`. Strings must be written within quotation marks. Usually, double quotes are used. However, single quotes may also be used. Consider the following code excerpt:

```
var person = "John James";      // double quotes
var areaName = 'Burj Khalifa';  // Using single quotes
```

It is also possible to use single quotes within a string that is written within double quotes. Consider the following example:

```
var text = "It's a rainy day";  // correct
```

Or you can use the following acceptable form:

```
var text = "My profession is 'Computer programmer'";  //correct
```

Likewise, you can use double quotes within a sting written within single quotes:

```
var text = 'My Profession is "Computer programmer" '; // correct
```

However the following examples are not acceptable and will generate a syntax error:

```
var text = 'My profession is 'Computer programmer''; // wrong
var text = "My profession is "Computer programmer'"'; // wrong
```

To make things a little more complicated, these two inadmissible forms may be adjusted slightly to avoid syntax errors. The single quote within the text must be preceded by a backslash. Now consider the same example:

```
var text = 'My Profession is \'Computer programmer\'  ' ; // correct
```

After execution of the statement, the variable text contains My Profession is 'Computer programmer'.

Likewise, the following statement is also acceptable:

```
var text = "My Profession is \"Computer programmer\"  " ; // correct
```

After execution, the variable text contains My Profession is "Computer programmer".

A string definition and assignment to a value may be in a single line or a set of lines. When using a string definition on multiple lines, you may use the escaped newline character (\n) like this:

```
var text = "My Profession is \nComputer programmer" ;
alert(text);
```

After execution of the preceding lines of code, the content of the variable text is displayed in the window as shown in Figure 2-2.

Figure 2-2. *String shown in two lines*

As shown, the text is composed of two lines. This is achieved by using \n in the string specification.

Another operator that you may use in the context of strings is +. Consider the following line of code:

```
var string1 = 'ABAP' + 'er' ; // string1 contains ABAPer
```

Adding the + operator results in the concatenation of the two sets of characters. The variable string1 will then contain "ABAPer". Now consider the following example:

```
var string1  = 1 + '7'; //
```

In this case, after execution of the statement, the string1 variable has the value "17". It results in a concatenation of the number 1 (also treated as a string) to the string '7' and the result in string1 is also a string.

Consider another example:

```
var string1  = 'A' + 1 + 7;  //  string1 will contain A17
```

In this case, when the statement is executed, the variable string1 will contain the value "A17" and not "A8". On the contrary, consider the following example:

```
var string1  = 1 + 7 + 'A' ;
```

After execution of this statement, the resulting value in string1 is "8A" and not "17A". The reason is that sequentially JavaScript treats 1 and 7 as numbers and performs addition until it encounters letter A. After this point, the computed value so far (8) is concatenated with A and stored in the variable string1. The type of the variable string1 is string.

Number

To represent number values, JavaScript has only one data type: number. The numbers may or may not have decimal places. In addition, they may or may not include unary operators. To clarify the usage of numbers within JS, let's consider a few examples.

The following line of code represents a whole number containing the value 26:

```
var num1 = 26;
```

Now consider another example:

```
var num2 = -26;
```

The variable num2 is assigned the value minus 26.

When defining variables in JavaScript, you do not need to specify the number of decimal places. When assigning variables, you must provide the corresponding value. Now let's consider a few examples of decimal numbers. The following are some examples of positive decimal values:

```
var num1 = 0.6888 ;
var num2 = 122.688;
var num3 = 10.0;
```

And you can also have a number with a minus sign and decimal places:

```
var num4 = -2.3;
```

You can also assign a number variable an exponential value. The following are some examples:

```
var num5 = 28.5e-3 ; //which is equal to .0285
var num6 = 28.5e3  ; //which is equal to 28500
```

This will store the value 2.78900 along with the necessary decimal places in the variable num1.
An addition operation may be performed:

```
var num1    = 2.78900 + 1 ;
```

When the addition is performed, the resulting value will be 3.789.

Within JS, there are two special numbers: positive infinity (infinity) and negative infinity (-infinity). A positive infinity results due to an arithmetic overflow within a program. On the other hand, a negative infinity occurs if you try to store (in a number variable) a value that is smaller than the allowed minimum value.

■ **Note** There are two special values, infinity and -infinity, that a number variable may contain.

Consider the following examples demonstrating that the number type is also used for storing hexadecimal and octal values. Hexadecimals values start with 0x:

```
var Hexval1 = -0xFFDD;
var Hexval2 =  0xFFDD;
```

Octal values start with a zero:

```
var Octval = 0628;
```

Undefined

If a variable has been declared but no value is assigned to it, that variable has the type undefined. Consider the following example:

```
var mytype ;
```

As you can see, this example declares the variable mytype, but no value has been assigned to it. The variable mytype has the type undefined.

```
var mytype ;   // mytype has undefined type
```

It is also possible to set a variable to undefined explicitly:

```
var mytype =  10;     // mytype has type number
mytype = undefined;   // now mytype has type undefined
```

Null

The null data type is used in JavaScript to explicitly specify that a variable has no value. You may simply assign null to a variable, as shown in this example:

```
var mytype = 1 ;
var mytype = null; // mytype has type null
```

■ **Note** When assigning null or undefined to a variable, do not include single or double quote marks around null or undefined. Otherwise, they will be treated as strings.

Object

The object data type within JavaScript represents a set of unordered properties and values. The syntax for defining an object within your program is as follows:

```
var myobj = { property1 :  val1 ,  property2 :val2 ...  property : valn };
```

Object definitions may be written on a single line or on multiple lines. The property and the respective value must be separated by a colon, whereas the property-value pairs are separated by commas. Within a program, an object is also a variable defined via the var keyword. However, an object is composed of a number of properties and values.

Consider this example:

```
var employee1 = { pernr :  '1', empName : "John Wright" ,  gender : 'M', country : "USA" } ;
```

This example defines an object named employee1 with properties empName, gender, and country, and assigns values to the various properties.

The same definition and assignment may be done in multiple lines:

```
var employee1 = {  pernr :  '1',
                   empName : "John Wright" ,
                   gender : 'M',
                   country : "USA" } ;
```

When defining an object, make sure that you use only curly brackets, { }, to enclose the properties and value pairs. Using parentheses to enclose them will generate a syntax error and is not allowed.

To address the various properties, use the dot operator:

```
alert ( employee1.pernr) ;
```

The preceding statement will display a dialog box with the value 1.

It is also possible to change the value of a particular property of a given object:

```
employee1.pernr = 2 ;
```

Once this is done, in the case of the employee1 object, the value of pernr will be 2.

You may assign a given object to another object as shown here:

```
var employee1 = { pernr :  '1', empName : "John Wright" ,  gender : 'M', country : "USA" } ;
var employee2 = employee1;
employee2.pernr = '2';
employee2.empName = 'James Dolman' ;

alert ( employee2.pernr + " " + employee2.empName + " " + employee2.gender + " " +
employee2.country ) ;
```

As you can see, this example first creates an object named employee1 and assigns appropriate property values for the employee John Wright having personnel number 1. Next, the object employee1 is assigned to the newly declared object employee2. The properties pernr and empName of object employee2 are changed and output in a dialog box using the alert function. The output of the program is shown in Figure 2-3.

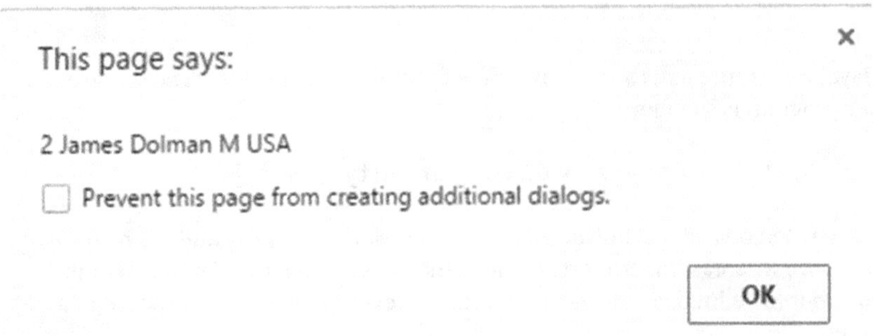

This page says: ✕

2 James Dolman M USA

☐ Prevent this page from creating additional dialogs.

OK

Figure 2-3. *Program output*

When specifying properties of objects, you may specify undefined or null as the value for a property. An example of specifying null is shown here:

```
var employee1 = { pernr : null, empName : null ,  gender : 'M', country : "USA" } ;
employee1.pernr = '2' ;
employee1.empName = 'John Reed' ;
```

In addition to the dot notation, there is another way of addressing the properties of the object in question. This is shown in the following line of code:

```
employee1["pernr"] = '2' ;  correct
```

This will assign the value '2' to the property pernr of the employee1 object. As you can see, the property name is enclosed in double quotes and square brackets. It is also possible to enclose the property name in single quotes. Consider the following statement, which has the same effect:

```
employee1['pernr']  = '2';   // correct
```

You must make sure, however, to use only square brackets with the single or double quotes, as shown in the examples. Using parentheses or curly brackets will produce a syntax error:

```
employee1('pernr') = '2' ;   // Wrong
```

In addition, omitting the quotes (either single or double), even when used in conjunction with the square brackets, is also problematic, as shown here:

```
employee1[ pernr ] = '2' ;   // Wrong
```

Objects Within Objects

Thus far you have seen examples of objects containing a set of properties only. Now you'll see how you can define objects that contain one or more other objects. You can achieve this by slightly modifying the previous employee1 example. Instead of using a property name based on a string, the modified example introduces a new property fullname that is based on an object having properties lastname and firstname. The code for this is as follows:

```
var employee1 = {  pernr :  '1',
                   fullname : { lastname : "John" , firstname : "Wright" } ,
                   gender : 'M',
                   country : "USA" } ;
```

Here, as in the original example, an object employee1 is defined that has a number of properties. However, employee1 now has a property named fullname, which itself is an object comprising properties lastname and firstname. Note the usage of curly brackets for the employee1 and fullname objects. Within the subobject, colons and commas are used in the same manner as they have been used in the main object specification.

Consider the examples described in the following sections.

■ **Note**   A special object known as an array exists in JavaScript. An array is an ordered set of values and is written within square brackets; e.g., [1,2,7,10] or ['my', 'she']. Arrays will be discussed in detail in Chapter 5 and subsequent chapters.

Boolean

As the name denotes, a variable based on the Boolean data type may have a value of either true or false. Consider the following:

```
var  bool1 =  true;  // correct
var  bool2 = false ; // correct
```

These examples define two Boolean variables, bool1 and bool2, and assign true and false values to them, respectively. Importantly, the assigned values cannot be written in single or double quotes, and must be written in lowercase letters.

■ **Note**   When you assign true and false to Boolean variables, make sure that you do not write them in single or double quotes. Otherwise, they will be treated as strings. Also make sure to use all lowercase.

Consider these examples:

```
var  bool1 =  "true";  // wrongly defined as string - not boolean
var  bool2 = "false" ; // wrongly defined as string - not boolean
```

Here, both bool1 and bool2 are strings and not Booleans.

Boolean variables are used in conditional evaluation, and may be used to store the result of a conditional evaluation, such as with if and while statements. (The statements are discussed in further detail in the latter part of the book). Consider the following line:

```
var boolean1 =  ( 10 > 1 ) ;
```

After execution of the script, the variable boolean1 contains the value true. Next, consider this example:

```
var boolean2 =  ( 0 > 1 ) ;
```

In this case, the boolean2 variable contains the value false.

The typeof Operator

An important operator in JavaScript is **typeof**. The typeof operator returns a string that denotes the type of the operand in question. The syntax of the typeof operator is shown here:

```
typeof (variable) ;
typeof variable ;
```

The variable or operand could belong to any of the types discussed in this chapter. If you use the typeof operator to evaluate a single operand in a single statement, you can omit the brackets that enclose the variable name. You may also use the typeof operator in the alert method or the console.log method (discussed in the next section).

The following example shows how the typeof operator is used:

```
var text = 'My Profession is "Computer programming" '.
alert (typeof(text));     //    string  displayed in dialog box
```

In this example, the typeof operator returns a string, and this is displayed in the dialog box.

Consider this code, in which the operator correctly returns the object type:

```
var employee1 = {  pernr :  '1',
fullname : { lastname : "John" , firstname : "Wright" } ,
            gender : 'M',
            country : "USA" } ;
alert (typeof(employee1) ) ; //  object displayed in dialog box
```

In the following code, variable boolean1 belongs to the Boolean data type. Hence, the typeof operator returns Boolean.

```
var boolean1 =  ( 10 > 1 ) ;
alert (typeof(boolean1)) ;    // boolean displayed in dialog box
```

As mentioned earlier, when a variable is declared but not assigned a value, the type of the variable is undefined. The same undefined type is determined by the typeof operator:

```
var mytype ;  // mytype has undefined type
alert (typeof(mytype)) ;   // undefined displayed in dialog box
```

The typeof operator also works with numbers and gives the correct type (i.e., number):

```
mytype = 10;  // mytype has type number
alert (typeof(mytype)) ;   // number displayed in dialog box
```

Finally, this example shows how the typeof operator behaves when null is involved:

```
mytype = 1 ;
mytype = null; // mytype has type null
alert(typeof( mytype)) ;  // but  object displayed in dialog box ----wrongly displayed
```

In the case of a null value, the typeof operator incorrectly returns the type name as object. The developer needs to be careful and write appropriate measures in order to deal with such situations.

■ **Caution**   The typeof operator returns the correct JS type in all cases except type null. In this case, it wrongly returns "object".

Method console.log

Thus far in the chapter you have seen the various available data types in JS along with some examples, including how to display information in a dialog box using the alert method. However, for testing and debugging purposes, you may need to display values of certain variables at various points during program execution.

■ **Note**   The console.log method is not recommended for an actual live environment. However, it must be used for testing while development of JS programs.

You can use the console.log method to display test values of variables while executing a program. Although coloring and stylizing options may be possible, here we will only cover the basic working of the method. Here's the syntax of this method:

```
console.log( obj1, obj2 ....objn );
```

The console.log method may take as input one or more numbers, strings, Boolean values, or objects. You may also display one or more properties of an object using the console.log method. You can also use console.log in conjunction with the typeof operator. For objects containing further objects, you can drill down into further details of the object.

■ **Note**   When the values passed to the console.log method involve an operation to be performed, such as addition or concatenation, the result is first computed and then output.

The following example shows the console.log method in action:

```
<!DOCTYPE html>
<html>
<body>
<h1>Console Log Demo </h1>
<script>
  console.log(10 + 5);
</script>
</body>
</html>
```

The Console object allows you to access the debugging console of the browser. The output of the console.log method is neither displayed with the rest of the web page content in the browser nor displayed in a pop-up box upon loading of the web page. Rather, it is displayed in the Console tab of the browser debugger. These are the steps to switch on the console display:

1. Open in a browser the web page containing the HTML and JavaScript code. (For purposes of this example, I'm using Google Chrome.)

2. Press Ctrl+Shift+I. This opens the debugger in a separate pane to the right of the web page output, as shown in Figure 2-4.

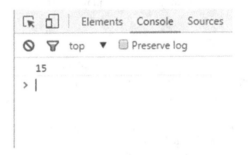

Figure 2-4. *Debugger Console tab*

3. Click the Console tab. You will now see the value displayed using the console. log method (in Figure 2-4, 15 is shown as a result of the addition).

■ **Note** Make sure that you write console.log in all lowercase letters in the JavaScript code. Writing it as Console.log will not give the desired result.

Consider the example presented in Listing 2-1.

Listing 2-1. Displaying Object employee1

```
<script>
var employee1 = {  pernr :  '1',
                   empName : "John Wright" ,
                   gender : 'M',
                   country : "USA" } ;

console.log(employee1);
</script>
```

Here, the employee1 object is passed as a parameter to the console.log method. The output in the console is shown in Figure 2-5.

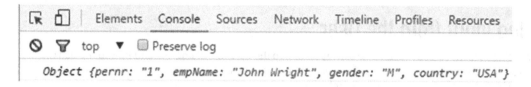

Figure 2-5. *Object employee1 displayed in console*

As you see, the object is displayed with the relevant properties and values in a single line.

Now consider an example where object employee1 includes a property fullname (which is another object):

```
var employee1 = {  pernr :  '1',
                   fullname : { lastname : "John" , firstname : "Wright" } ,
                   gender : 'M'',
                   country : "USA" } ;
console.log (employee1) ;
```

For nested objects such as this, the console output appears as shown in Figure 2-6.

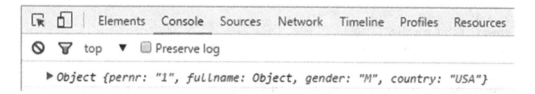

Figure 2-6. *Object employee1 displayed in Console*

In this case, no values are shown for the fullname property. Rather, only Object is displayed for it. You can expand the Object node to see the full details of employee1, as shown in Figure 2-7.

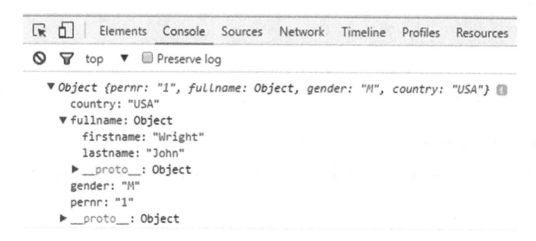

Figure 2-7. *Expanded object employee1*

As you can see, in the detailed view within the Chrome console, the properties are listed in alphabetical order.

Taking Input from the User

So far in this chapter, you have seen how to output data to the user in a dialog box and how to debug your web pages in the web browser console. Now you will see how you can take input from the user viewing the web page in which your JavaScript code is embedded.

The prompt method of the Window object is used for this purpose, as shown in the following syntax:

```
window.prompt ( text , optional default text ) ;
prompt ( text , optional default text ) ;
```

The call of the prompt method takes as input the text that is displayed to the user, as well as an optional default value. A dialog box is displayed on the web page. This is a *modal* dialog box, meaning it will not allow the user to perform any other activity in the browser until the dialog box is closed. The dialog box is displayed with two buttons, OK and Cancel.

You may assign the text entered by the user to a variable declared in your program. Irrespective of the type of the variable used, after the user enters a value in the dialog box input field and clicks the OK button, the type of the returning variable becomes string.

To better understand, consider the following example:

```
var value  = 0;
value = prompt("Enter a value", "10") ;
alert('You entered ' + value + ' which has type '  + typeof(value)  );
```

This example specifies a number variable value and then calls the prompt method of the window object and assigns the inputted value to the variable. A default text of 10 is specified in the method call. The example then uses an alert method to display the entered value and its type in another dialog box. The input dialog box that this code generates is shown in Figure 2-8.

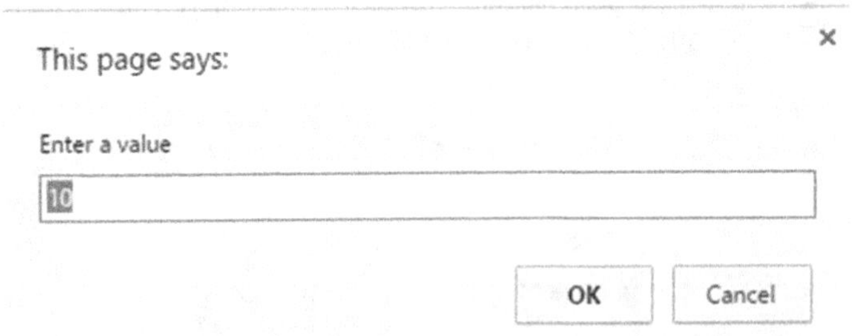

Figure 2-8. Input dialog box

When the user enters a value such as 10 and clicks OK, the message is displayed as shown in Figure 2-9.

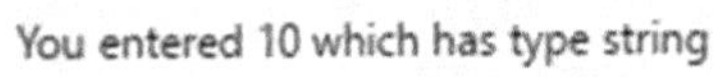

Figure 2-9. Message displayed

28

As you can see, the variable value is assigned the value 10 and the type of the value entered is interpreted as a string.

If, on the other hand, the user clicks the Cancel button, the variable value will be assigned null.

Commonly Used Keywords in JavaScript

To conclude the chapter, Table 2-4 presents a list of some keywords (reserved words) in the JavaScript language. Please note that you are not allowed to define variables that have the same names as these keywords, which is why they are called reserved.

Table 2-4. *Reserved Words*

Boolean	break	case
catch	class	continue
default	do	else
false	final	for
function	if	in
instanceof	int	new
null	private	protected
public	return	short
static	super	switch
this	throw	true
try	typeof	var
while	with	

Summary

In this chapter, you were introduced to the Window object and the data types that JavaScript provides. Next, you saw how to display data to the user in a dialog box, debug your web page in the console of the browser, and take input from the user via a dialog box. The end of the chapter listed reserved words of the JS language.

Chapter 3 presents more detailed aspects of JavaScript. You will see the various control structures in the JS language and how to use them to sfulfill requirements.

■ ■ ■

Operators in JavaScript

This chapter explains JavaScript operators in detail. It starts with the arithmetic operators and then looks at the comparison operators and logical operators that are used for formulating conditional checks in JS programs. The final section of the chapter covers the assignment and bitwise operators.

Arithmetic Operators

Arithmetic operators take values in the form of literals or variables as operands and return a single value. The standard arithmetic operators supported in JavaScript are listed in Table 3-1. Each is described in turn in the subsections that follow.

Table 3-1. *Arithmetic Operators*

Operator Description	Operator
Addition	+
Subtraction	-
Multiplication	*
Division	/
Remainder (modulo or modulus)	%
Exponentiation	**
Increment	++
Decrement	- -
Unary negation	-

Addition Operator

The addition operator (+) results in the addition (sum) of numeric operands. For strings, the addition operation results in string concatenation. The syntax of this is shown as follows:

```
A + B
```

© Rehan Zaidi 2017

R. Zaidi, *JavaScript Essentials for SAP ABAP Developers*, DOI 10.1007/978-1-4842-2220-1_3

The following are a few examples of the addition operator in action:

```
2 + 4                  //   6     addition performed
10 + "text"            //   10text concatenation
"text" + "string"      //   "textstring"
2 + true               //   results  in value 3
1 + false              //   1
```

Subtraction Operator

The subtraction operator (-) performs arithmetic subtraction of the two operands. The syntax is

```
x - y
```

In case of numeric operands, the difference between x and y is returned. In case of strings, the value NaN (not a number) is returned. The following are some examples of the subtraction operator in action:

```
10 - 6  // 4
6 - 10 // -4
"text" - 2 // NaN
```

Multiplication Operator

The multiplication operator (*) determines the product of the supplied operands. The syntax is

```
A * B
```

Examples of the multiplication operator include the following:

```
52 * 2 // results in 104
-22 * 2 // -44
Infinity * Infinity // Infinity
"abc" * 3 // NaN
```

Division Operator

The division operator (/) results in the quotient of the supplied operands. The syntax is

```
A / B
```

Here, the left operand (A) is the dividend and the right operand (B) is the divisor. Some examples of this operator include

```
1 / 2      // returns 0.5 in JavaScript
3 / 0      // returns Infinity in JavaScript
3.0 / -0.0 // returns -Infinity in JavaScript
```

Remainder Operator

The remainder (or modulo) operator (%) is used for determining the leftover (remainder) when the first operand is divided by the second. The remainder always has the sign of the dividend. The syntax is

```
A % B
```

The math of the reminder operator is less straightforward, so several examples of its usage are provided here:

```
result = ( 13 % 4 ); //    1
result = ( -1 % 3 ); //   -1
result = ( 1 % -3 ); //    1
result = ( 1 % 3 );  //    1
result = ( 2 % 6 );  //    2
result = ( -6 % 2 ); //   -0
result = ( 6.5 % 2) ; //    0.5
```

Exponentiation Operator

The exponentiation operator (**) is used for raising the first operand to the power of the second. The syntax is

```
A ** B
```

The following are some examples of the exponentiation operator:

```
2 ** 4 // 16
4 ** 4 // 256
10 ** -2 // 0.01
```

Increment Operator

The increment operator (++) adds one to the value of the operand in question. The increment operator can have either of two forms, postfix or prefix.

The syntax of the postfix form is

```
A++
```

In this form, the variable A is first returned and then incremented.
The syntax of the prefix form is

```
++A
```

In the prefix form, the variable A is first incremented before being returned.
The following are examples of both forms of the increment operator:

```
// Postfix
var A = 6;
B = A++; // after this, B = 6, A = 7
```

```
// Prefix
var A = 6;
B = ++A; // after this, A = 6, B = 6
```

Decrement Operator

The decrement operator (--) decreases its operand value by one (i.e., deducts one from the value). Like the increment operator, the decrement operator can have either of two forms, postfix or prefix.

The syntax of the postfix form is

```
A--
```

In the postfix form, the variable A is first returned and then decremented.

The syntax of the prefix form is

```
--A
```

In the prefix form, the variable A is first decremented before being returned.

The following are examples of both forms of the decrement operator:

```
// Postfix
var A = 6;
var B = A--; // B = 6, A = 5

// Prefix
var A = 6;
var B = --A; // A = 5, B = 5
```

Unary Negation Operator

The unary negation operator (-) precedes the operand in question, and when used within expressions, negates its value. Consider the following example:

```
// unary negation
var A = 6;
B = -A; // B = -6          A = 6
```

In this example, after the execution of the statement, the variable B contains the value -6, whereas the value of A still remains 6.

Comparison Operators

JavaScript supports a variety of comparison operators, all of which are explained in the following subsections.

Greater Than Operator

The greater than (>) operator checks whether the value of the left operand is greater than that of the right operand. If it is, the condition returns true. Otherwise, it returns false. The syntax is

```
A > B
```

Less Than Operator

As the name indicates, the less than operator (<) checks whether the value of the left operand is less than that of the right operand. If it is, the condition returns true. Otherwise, it returns false. The syntax is

```
A < B
```

Greater Than or Equal To Operator

The condition using the greater than or equal to operator (>=) is true when the value of the left operand is greater than or equal to the value of the operand on the right. Otherwise, it is false. The syntax is

```
A >= B
```

▓ **Note**   Strings are compared based on lexicographical ordering.

Less Than or Equal To Operator

The condition using the less than or equal to operator (<=) is true when the value of the left operand is greater than or equal to the value of the operand on the right. Otherwise, it is false. The syntax is

```
A <= B
```

Listing 3-1 shows how to use the JS comparison operators discussed so far.

Listing 3-1. Operator Usage Example 1

```html
<html>
  <body>

    <script >

            var a = 20;
            var b = 30;
            var result;

            console.log("(a < b) returned ");
            result = (a < b);
            console.log(result);
```

```
        console.log("(a > b) returned   ");
        result = (a > b);
        console.log(result);

        console.log ("(a >= b) returned ");
        result = (a >= b);
        console.log (result);

        console.log ("(a <= b) returned ");
        result = (a <= b);
        console.log (result);

    </script>
  </body>
</html>
```

When the preceding program is executed, the output in the browser console appears as shown in Figure 3-1.

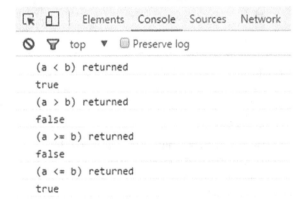

Figure 3-1. *Program output*

The variables a and b are assigned values 20 and 30, respectively. The output of the condition is returned in the variable result.

Equality and Inequality Operators

This section discusses four available comparison operators related to testing equality and inequality. It also presents code examples to help you better understand their usage.

■ **Note**   JavaScript supports both strict and type–converting comparisons.

Equality Operator

The equality operator (==) returns true if the two operands involved are equal. Before the comparison, the operator applies operand conversion in case the two operands are not of the same type.

```
6   ==  6          // true
"6"  ==  6          // true
0   == false       // true
0   == null        // false
null == undefined // true
true == 1          // true
```

Inequality Operator

The inequality operator (!=) returns true if the two operands involved are not equal. Before the comparison, the operator applies operand conversion in case the two operands are not of the same type.

```
6 != 6      // false
6 != "6"    // false
0 != false  // false
```

Strict Equality (Identity) Operator

The strict equality operator (===) returns true if the two operands in question are structural equal without any type conversion. The syntax is

```
A === B
```

When two strings are compared using this operator, a value of true is only returned when they have the same sequence of characters and same length.

For the comparison of two numbers, the === operator succeeds when they have the same numeric value. Two Booleans are strictly equal if either both of them are true or both of them are false.

```
8 === 8   // true
8 === '8' // false
'Abc'  === 'Abc'  // true
```

Non-identity/Strict Inequality Operator

The non-identity operator (!==) returns true in either of the following cases:

- The two operands are not equal.

- The two operands are not of the same type.

The syntax of non-identity operator is

```
A !== B
```

Consider the following example of the non-identity operator:

```
6 !== '6' // true
6 !== 3   // true
```

Logical Operators

Like many other programming languages, JavaScript supports several logical operators. Logical operators are used in expressions to formulate conditions. They return a value of either true or false after evaluation. However, when used with non-Boolean values, they may return a non-Boolean value. Table 3-2 shows the three logical operators supported in JS.

Table 3-2. Logical Operators

Operator	Example	Effect
AND(&&)	ex1 && ex2	When used with Booleans, && returns true if both operands ex1 and ex2 are true.
OR (||)	ex1 || ex2	When used with Booleans, || returns true when at least one operand is true. In case both ex1 and ex2 are false, || operator returns false.
NOT (!)	!ex1	This results in false when the operand in question is convertible true; otherwise, the expression returns true.

Now that you have an idea of the three logical operators available, let's take a look at a few full-fledged working examples. Consider the code in Listing 3-2 that uses the && operator.

Listing 3-2. Example of Logical Operators

```
var result;

result = (true && true);
console.log("( true && true ) returns ", result);

result = ( false && true);
console.log("( false && true ) returns  ", result);

result = (false && false );
console.log ("( false && false ) returns ", result);

result = ( 'a' && 'b');
console.log ("( a && b ) returns ", result);

result = ( false && 'a' );
console.log ("( false && a ) returns ", result);

result = 'a' && true;
console.log ("( a && true ) returns ", result);
```

This example uses the && operator on a number of operands, including Boolean and non-Boolean. The output of Listing 3-2 in the web browser console is shown in Figure 3-2.

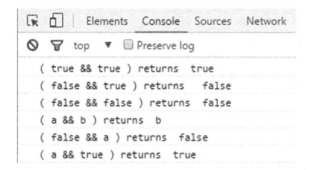

Figure 3-2. *Program output*

As you can see, when Booleans are involved, the result is always a Boolean value. However, non-Boolean operands give strange results. Listing 3-3 shows an example involving the logical OR and NOT operators.

Listing 3-3. Usage of Logical AND and NOT Operators

```
var result;

result = (true || true);
console.log("( true || true ) returns ", result);
result = (false || true);
console.log("( false || true ) returns ", result);
result = (false || (6 >= 4 ) );
console.log("( false || (6 >= 4 ) ) returns ", result);
result = ( 'a' || D );
console.log("( a || D ) returns ", result);
result = ( false || 'a' );
console.log("( false || a ) returns ", result);
result = ( ! false );
console.log("( ! false ) returns ", result);
result = ( ! true );
console.log("( ! true ) returns ", result);
```

The output of Listing 3-3 is shown in Figure 3-3.

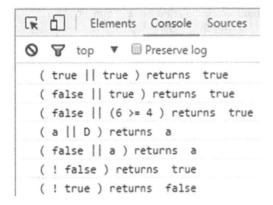

Figure 3-3. *Output showing AND and NOT operators*

This example uses both Boolean and non-Boolean values with the operators. In the case of non-Boolean values, a non-Boolean value is the result of the operator usage.

Logical expressions are evaluated left to right. When an expression that is true is "ORed" with any other expression(s), JS evaluates the entire thing as true without performing any subsequent evaluations:

```
true || any_expression        evaluated as      true
```

On the other hand, when a false expression is "ANDed" with any number of expressions, the logical operation returns false:

```
false && any_expression        evaluated as      false
```

This is known as *short-circuit evaluation* (or McCarthy evaluation).

Bitwise Operators

JavaScript also supports a number of bitwise operators. Bitwise operators consider their operands as signed 32-bit sequences, in two's complement, comprising ones and zeros (i.e., binary representation) rather than decimals or hexadecimals. However, once the operator function has been performed, JS number values are returned. The various bitwise operators are shown in Table 3-3.

Table 3-3. *Bitwise Operators*

Operator Description	Operator
AND	&
OR	|
XOR	^
NOT	~
Shift left	<<
Signed shift right (sign-propagating right shift)	>>
Unsigned shift right (zero-fill right shift)	>>>

In order to use these operators, you have to understand how the operands are stored and interpreted. For all the operators in Table 3-3, the operands are treated as 32-bit binary numbers, and then the respective operation is applied on one or more operands. In this format, the leftmost bit is the sign bit. This bit is either 1 or 0. A 0 indicates a positive number, whereas a 1 indicates that the number is negative.

Let's examine two examples, one positive and one negative, and how they are represented as 32-bit binary number values. First, let's see how a positive number is stored. For example, the number +10 is represented as

```
00000000 00000000 00000000 00001010
```

On the other hand, the number +2 is shown as

```
00000000 00000000 00000000 00000010
```

Now let's see how a negative number is stored. The number -11 is stored as follows:

```
11111111 11111111 11111111 11110101          =     -11
```

Bitwise AND

The Bitwise AND operator (&) carries out an AND operation on each bit of the two operands (i.e., their 32-bit representation). If the corresponding bits of two operands are equal to 1, this results in a 1 in the corresponding bit of the result. Otherwise, the resulting bit is set to 0.

The syntax is

```
A & B;
```

In the following case, the two numbers (2 and 10) are ANDed:

```
var num = 2 & 10 ;  // result is number 2
```

Let's look at how this works. The following shows the 32-bit binary representation of the numbers 2 and 10, and the resulting number after the bitwise AND operation:

```
00000000 00000000 00000000 00000010          =     2
00000000 00000000 00000000 00001010          =     10
---------------------------------------------------------------
00000000 00000000 00000000 00000010          =     2     =  2 & 10
```

As you can see, the rightmost bits of the two operands are equal to 0, so the result contains 0 as well in the corresponding place. Because both the operands contain a 1 at the second-to-last bit position, the resulting bit is set as 1 after the AND operation.

Bitwise OR

The bitwise OR operator (|) carries out an OR on each bit of the two 32-bit number equivalent operands. If at least one of the bits is found to be 1, this results in a 1 in the corresponding bit of the result. Otherwise, the resulting bit is set to 0. The syntax is

```
A | B;
```

An example of the bitwise OR operator is shown here:

```
var num = 2 | 10 ;  // result is 10
```

The following shows the 32-bit binary representation of the numbers, and the resulting number after the bitwise OR operation:

```
00000000 00000000 00000000 00000010                =    2
00000000 00000000 00000000 00001010                =    10
-----------------------------------------------------------
00000000 00000000 00000000 00001010                =    10   =  2 | 10
```

As you can see, the rightmost bits of the two operands are equal to 0, so the result contains 0 as well in the corresponding place. Because both the operands contain a 1 at the second-to-last bit position, the resulting bit is set as 1 after the OR operation. The position where at least one bit (in either the first or second operand) is equal to 1, the resulting bit is also set as 1.

Bitwise XOR

The bitwise exclusive OR, or XOR, operator (^) is somewhat similar to the OR operator. The bit in the resulting number is set to 1 only when one of the bits in the operand is 1 and the other one is 0. When only one of the bits is found to be 1, this results in a 0 in the corresponding bit of the result. In all other cases, the resulting bit is set to 0. The syntax is

```
A ^ B;
```

Here's an example of the XOR operator:

```
var num = 2 ^ 10 ;
```

Let's look at how this works. The following shows the 32-bit binary representation of the numbers 2 and 10, and the resulting number after the bitwise XOR operation:

```
00000000 00000000 00000000 00000010                =    2
00000000 00000000 00000000 00001010                =    10
-----------------------------------------------------------
00000000 00000000 00000000 00001000                =    8    =  2 ^ 10
```

As you can see, the rightmost bits of the two operands are equal to 0, so the result contains 0 as well in the corresponding place. Because both the operands contain a 1 at the second-to-last bit position, the resulting bit is set as a 0 after the exclusive OR operation.

Bitwise NOT

The bitwise NOT operator (~) is a unary operator, meaning it involves only one operand. It simply negates the bits in the operand. Every 0 bit becomes 1 and vice versa. The syntax is

```
~ A
```

Here's an example of the bitwise NOT operator:

```
var num = ~ 10;
```

The following shows the 32-bit binary representation of the number 3, and the resulting number after the NOT operation:

```
00000000 00000000 00000000 00001010          =     10

----------------------------------------------------------------
11111111 11111111 11111111 11110101          =     -11   =   ~ 10
```

As you can see, the NOT operation reversed all the bits of the operand, including the sign bit. This results in a value of -11.

To summarize what has been discussed thus far, Table 3-4 presents a truth table that shows the various bitwise operators.

Table 3-4. *Truth Table for AND, OR, and XOR Operators*

Bit in Operand A	Bit in Operand B	Resulting Bit after AND	Resulting Bit after OR	Resulting Bit after XOR
0	0	0	0	0
0	1	0	1	1
1	0	0	1	1
1	1	1	1	0

Bitwise Left Shift

As the name indicates, the bitwise left shift operator (<<) shifts the bits of the given operand to the left. You specify the number of bits to be shifted via the operand B. Bits comprising of zeros equal to the number of shifted places are added to the right of operand A. The syntax of the left shift operator is

```
A << B
```

Consider the following example:

```
var result = ( 10  << 2  ); // left shift by two places
```

In this case, the number 10 before shifting is shown as

```
00000000 00000000 00000000 00001010
```

After shifting it two places to the left, the binary representation looks like this:

```
00000000 00000000 00000000 00101000
```

Two zeros have been added to the left. This result now is the decimal number 40.

Bitwise Unsigned Right Shift

The bitwise unsigned right shift operator (>>>) is also known as zero-fill right shift. No matter what is the sign of the operand, it always results in a non-negative value. The syntax is

```
A >>> B ;
```

It shifts the bits of the operand A by the number of places specified by B. The bits that are shifted to the right are lost these are equal to B). On the left side, zeros are added equal to the number of places shifted (i.e., B). After the operation, the leftmost bit is always equal to zero (i.e., results in a non-negative value). Consider the following example:

```
var result = ( 10  >>> 2  ); // right shift by two places
```

In this case, the number 10 before shifting is shown here:

```
00000000 00000000 00000000 00001010
```

After shifting it two places to the right, the binary representation looks like this:

```
00000000 00000000 00000000 00000010
```

To the left, two zeros have been added. This result now is the decimal number 2.

Bitwise Signed Right Shift

The bitwise signed shift right operator (>>), also known as sign-propagating right shift, shifts the bits to the right. However, the sign of the number is also preserved. The number of places that are moved to the right are filled by the sign bit whether zero or 1. The syntax is

```
A >> B ;
```

Consider the following example:

```
var result = ( -10 >> 2 ); //  signed right shift  result  = -3
```

In this code, after the execution of the statement, the result variable contains the value -3.

Coding Example

Now that you are familiar with the various bitwise operators, Listing 3-4 shows a full-fledged coding example.

Listing 3-4. Example for Bitwise Operators

```
var result;
result = ( 2 & 10 ); //  AND
console.log("( 2 AND 10 ) returns ", result);
```

```
result = ( 10 | 2 ); // OR
console.log("( 10 OR 2 ) returns  ", result);

result = ( 10 ^ 2 ); // XOR
console.log ("( 10 XOR 2 ) returns ", result);

result = ( ~ 10 );  // NOT
console.log ("( NOT 10 ) returns ", result);

result = ( 10  << 2  ); // left shift by two
console.log("( 10  << 2  ) returns  ", result);

result = ( -10 >> 2 ); //  signed right shift
console.log ("( -10 >> 2 ) returns ", result);

result = ( 10 >>> 2 );  // unsigned right shift
console.log ("( 10 >>> 2 ) returns ", result);
```

The output of this program is shown in Figure 3-4.

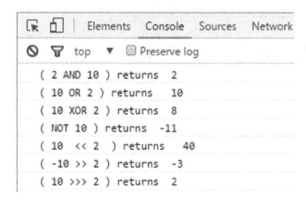

Figure 3-4. *Program output*

Assignment Operators

JavaScript also supports a number of assignment operators. An *assignment operator* may be simply defined as an operator that "assigns" value to the left operand considering the value of the right operand.

The various assignment operators are shown in Table 3-5.

Table 3-5. *Assignment Operators*

Operator	Operator Usage/Shorthand	Actual Effect
Assignment (basic assignment)	x = y	x = y
Addition assignment	x += y	x = x + y
Subtraction assignment	x -= y	x = x - y
Multiplication assignment	x *= y	x = x * y
Division assignment	x /= y	x = x / y
Remainder assignment	x %= y	x = x % y
Exponentiation assignment	x **= y	x = x ** y
Left shift assignment	x <<= y	x = x << y
Right shift assignment	x >>= y	x = x >> y
Unsigned right shift assignment	x >>>= y	x = x >>> y
Bitwise AND assignment	x &= y	x = x & y
Bitwise XOR assignment	x ^= y	x = x ^ y
Bitwise OR assignment	x |= y	x = x | y

As you are aware, the basic assignment operator (=) assigns the value of the right operand to the one on the left. The rest of the operators are shorthand for the various operators discussed so far in this chapter. For example, consider the following:

```
x &= y
```

This code is simply a shorthand equivalent to the following:

```
x = x & y
```

Consider the following block of code:

```
var result = 2;
result  &=  10;
```

This code is the same as

```
var result = 2 & 10;
```

Make sure, however, that there are no spaces within the assignment operator used, in this case &=. Writing it as & = will produce a syntax error.

String Operator

So far in this chapter, you have seen the operator + used as an arithmetic operator. However, when used with strings, the + operator behaves as a string operator that provides the concatenation functionality. In Chapter 2, you saw numerous examples of this when used with numbers and/or strings.

Summary

This chapter first explained the arithmetic operators provided by JavaScript in detail. It then covered the usage of the comparison and logical operators, followed by a detailed explanation of the bitwise operators. Finally, you saw the various assignment operators that are used as shorthand for the various bitwise, logical, and arithmetic operators supported by JavaScript. The journey of the JavaScript learning goes on, and in the next chapter you will see in detail the control structures that are mainly used within the JS arena.

CHAPTER 4

Control Structures in JavaScript

This chapter describes the various control structures in the JS language and demonstrates how to use them to fulfill requirements. The chapter begins with an overview of the block statements supported in JavaScript. Next, the if...else and the switch statements are covered in detail. You will then be introduced to the various types of loops supported in JavaScript, including the for and while loops, and given demo programs showing how to execute them. The chapter wraps up with brief coverage of the LABEL statement.

Block Statement

A block is used for grouping a set of statements. A block is enclosed within a pair of curly brackets, {}. The basic syntax is

```
{
  st_1;
  st_2;
}
```

Block statements are used within the various control structures. These include the if statement and the while and for loops (covered in the latter part of this chapter). Consider the following example:

```
var abc = 0;
while ( abc < 122) {
  abc = abc + 2;
}
```

Within this block of code, {abc = abc + 2;} is the block statement.
Consider another example of a block:

```
var abc = 150;
{
  var abc = 100 + 2;
}
alert(abc); // outputs 102
```

This code outputs 102 because the second var statement (inside the curly brackets) lies in the same scope as the var statement prior to the block.

© Rehan Zaidi 2017
R. Zaidi, *JavaScript Essentials for SAP ABAP Developers*, DOI 10.1007/978-1-4842-2220-1_4

Listing 4-1 shows an example of using compound statements within a block.

Listing 4-1. Block Example

```
<html>
   <body>
      <script>
         {
         var x = 5;
         x++;
         }
         console.log(x);
      </script>
   </body>
</html>
```

The output of the program is shown in Figure 4-1.

Figure 4-1. Block output

Conditional Statements

JavaScript provides two conditional statements:

- if...else
- switch

These statements let you execute a block of code when a given condition is found to be true. Or, in the case of an if statement, it may be possible to execute a statement block when a condition is found to be false.

if...else Statement

An if statement executes a set of statements when a logical condition is found to be true. An optional else clause is used to execute statements when the condition is determined to be false. The flowchart pertaining to a simple if statement is shown in Figure 4-2.

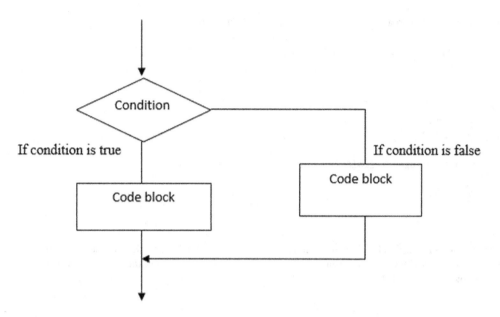

Figure 4-2. *Flowchart of if statement*

The syntax of an if statement is

```
if (eval_of_condition) {
  first_block;
} else {
  second_block;
}
```

Any expression that results in true or false may be used to formulate the condition. If the condition is found to be true, first_block is executed; otherwise, second_block is executed. The block may contain any number of statements, including further if statements.

It is also possible to specify multiple conditions to be checked one by one using if and else if to have multiple conditions tested in sequence, as follows:

```
if (eval_cond1) {
  block_1;
} else if (eval_cond2) {
  block_2;
} else if (eval_cond3) {
  block_3;
} else {
  last_block;
}
```

When multiple conditions are specified, the code pertaining to the first condition that evaluates to true will be executed. If the first condition is found to be false, the next condition specified by else if is checked, and then the next else if, and so on. If all three conditions are false, the last_block code is executed.

■ **Note**   The values false, null, undefined, and 0 when evaluated always result in a "false" value.

Listing 4-2 shows how to create a short program using an if statement.

Listing 4-2. Driving License Program Using if Statement

```
<html>
  <body>
    <script>
      var age = 20;
      if( age > 18 )
        {
            console.log("Eligible for Driving license");
        }
    </script>
  </body>
</html>
```

The example shows a simple if statement. The variable age with value 20 is declared. The condition in the if statement states that if age is greater than 18, then the code block should be executed. The output of this program is shown in Figure 4-3.

Eligible for Driving license

Figure 4-3. *Program output*

Listing 4-3 complicates things a bit by changing the example to add an else clause.

Listing 4-3. Driving License Program with else Clause

```
<html>
  <body>
    <script>
        var age = 18;
        if( age > 18 ){
            console.log("Eligible for Driving license");
        }
        else if( age == 18 ){
            console.log("Eligible for learning license");
        }
        else{
            console.log("Not eligible for Driving license");
        }
    </script>
  </body>
<html>
```

In this case, the block of code pertaining to the satisfied condition is executed, and the corresponding output is printed via the console.log statement. In this example, the else if condition (i.e., age == 18) is satisfied, hence the output will be Eligible for learning license, as shown in Figure 4-4.

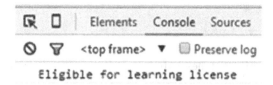

Figure 4-4. Program output

switch Statement

The switch statement enables you to evaluate an expression and then match its value using a number of case labels. When a match is found, the relevant code block is executed.

A break statement is used within the switch control structure. The break statement ensures that the program breaks out of switch once the expression is matched.

The flowchart of a switch control structure is shown in Figure 4-5.

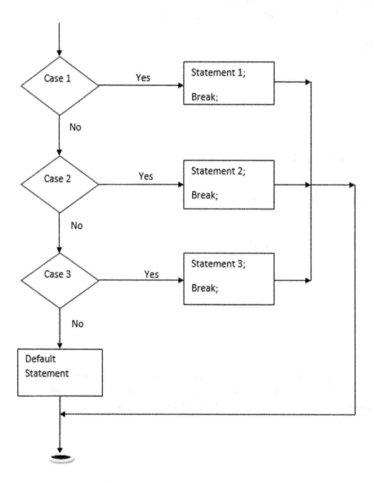

Figure 4-5. Flowchart of switch control structure

The syntax of a switch control structure is

```
switch (expression) {
  case value1:
    //Statements executed when the result of expression matches value1
    [break;]
  case value2:
    //Statements executed when the result of expression matches value2
    [break;]
  ...
  default:
    //Statements executed when none of the values match the value of the expression
    [break;]
}
```

The expression's resulting value is matched against each case value. If none of the case values match with that of the expression, then the default block code is executed.

Listing 4-4 provides an example of a switch statement in the driving license program.

Listing 4-4. switch Statement Example

```
<html>
<body>
<script>
var age = "16";
switch (age) {
    case "18":
        console.log("Eligible for learning license")
        break;
    case "20":
        console.log("Eligible for two wheeler license")
        break;
    case "23":
        console.log("Eligible for four wheeler license")
        break;
    default:
    console.log("Not eligible for license");
}
</script>
</body>
</html>
```

Variable age is declared with a value of 16 years. Different case clauses are included with respective coding. Listing 4-4 also includes a default clause to specify what the program should do if none of the values (specified via case clauses) are matched. Because the age is 16, the default code is executed. The output of the program is shown in Figure 4-6.

Figure 4-6. *Switch statement output*

As mentioned earlier, correct execution of the switch control structure requires the break statement. Listing 4-5 shows an example of a switch control structure without a break statement.

Listing 4-5. Example of Incorrect switch Control Structure

```
<!DOCTYPE html>
<html>
<body>
<script>
var color = "Green";
switch (color) {
    case "Red":
        console.log("Sign for Danger");
    case "Green":
        console.log("Sign for Growth");
    case "White":
        console.log("Sign for Peace");
    default:
    console.log("No sign");
}
</script>
</body>
</html>
```

Because the break statement has been omitted in Listing 4-5, the output is incorrectly displayed, as shown in Figure 4-7.

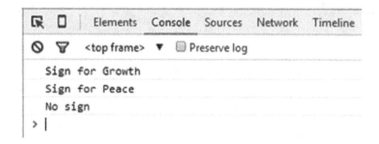

Figure 4-7. *Wrong output*

The value supplied to the switch expression is Green. This matches the second case clause, so only Sign for Growth should be displayed in the console log. However, because no break statement is included, after the execution of the matched statement, the two subsequent case clauses are also executed.

Loops in JavaScript

A loop helps to execute a block of code a number of times or repeatedly until a given condition is true. There are various types of loops supported in JS:

- while loop
- do...while loop
- for loop
- for...in loop

while Loop

This is a conditional loop. The while loop executes a block of code until the specified condition evaluates to true. As soon as the condition fails, the loop is stopped. The flowchart of the while loop is shown in Figure 4-8.

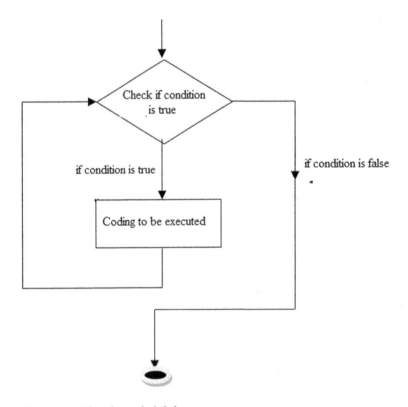

Figure 4-8. *Flowchart of while loop*

The generic syntax of the while loop is

```
while (condition)
{
    Statements to be executed if condition is true
}
```

Listing 4-6 provides a fully working example of a while loop.

Listing 4-6. while Loop Example

```
<html>
    <body>
        <script>
            var n = 0;
            console.log("Starting Loop ");
          while (n < 3)
        {
            console.log("Current Count : " + n + " ");
            n++;
        }
        console.log("Loop stopped!");
        </script>
    </body>
</html>
```

Listing 4-6 declares the variable n and assigns it a value of 0. The while loop condition states that the variable n should be less than 3. Within the loop, n is incremented by 1. Hence, the loop continues three times; that is, for n equals to 0, 1, and 2. As soon as the value of n equals 3 (i.e., the condition is satisfied), the loop stops.

The output of the program is shown in Figure 4-9.

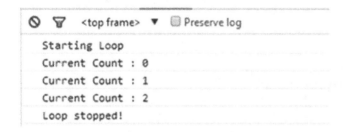

Figure 4-9. *Output of while loop*

do...while Loop

The do...while loop repeats until the specified condition is evaluated to false. The block of code is specified first and then the relevant condition is executed. This means that the loop will always be executed at least once, even if the condition is false. The flowchart is shown in Figure 4-10.

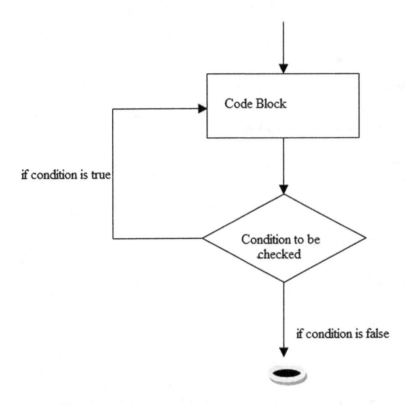

Figure 4-10. *Flowchart of do...while loop*

The syntax of the do...while loop is

```
do
{
   //Statements;
}
while (condition);
```

An example of the do...while loop is shown in Listing 4-7.

Listing 4-7. do...while Example

```
<html>
   <body>
      <script>
            var n = 0;
            console.log("Starting Loop ");
          do
        {
            console.log("Current Count : " + n + "");
            n++;
        }
```

```
         while (n < 4)
         console.log("Loop stopped!");
         </script>
     </body>
</html>
```

In this example, the value of the variable n is set to 0. On each loop iteration, the value of n is incremented by 1. The while loop reiterates until the value of n is no longer less than 4 (i.e., n equals 4).

The output of Listing 4-7 is shown in Figure 4-11.

```
◎  ▽   <top frame>  ▼  ▢ Preserve log

 Starting Loop
 Current Count : 0
 Current Count : 1
 Current Count : 2
 Current Count : 3
 Loop stopped!
```

Figure 4-11. *Output of do...while loop*

for Loop

The for loop is a conditional loop that continues until the specified condition evaluates to false. The generic syntax is

```
for ([initialization]; [test condition]; [expression])
{
    Statement
}
```

Within the initialization portion, you initialize the loop counter to a starting value. For the test condition you specify the condition that must be checked to determine whether or not the loop should continue. The expression is the part where you increase or decrease the counter or value.

Listing 4-8 shows an example of the for loop being used in a program.

Listing 4-8. for Loop Example

```
<html>
    <body>
        <script>
            var count;
            console.log("Starting Loop" + "");
            for(count = 0; count < 10; count++){
                console.log("Current Count : " + count );
            }
            console.log("Loop stopped!");
        </script>
    </body>
</html>
```

This example declares the variable count and then initializes the value of count to 0 in the for loop. Then, the loop condition checks whether the count value is less than 10. If so, the counter is incremented by 1.

Within the loop iteration, the current value of count is displayed. After each loop iteration, the count value is incremented by one and its value is checked based on the condition specified.

This loop runs ten times (for count equal to 0 to 9). When the value of count is equal to 10, the condition evaluates to false and the loop is stopped.

The output of the program is shown in Figure 4-12.

```
Starting Loop
Current Count : 0
Current Count : 1
Current Count : 2
Current Count : 3
Current Count : 4
Current Count : 5
Current Count : 6
Current Count : 7
Current Count : 8
Current Count : 9
Loop stopped!
```

Figure 4-12. *Program output*

The previous example showed you how to use a for loop to increment the counter value. Listing 4-9 presents another for loop example that shows you how to decrement the counter value.

Listing 4-9. Reverse for Loop

```html
<html>
    <body>
        <script>
                var count;
                console.log("Starting Loop" + "");
                for(count = 10 ; count > 0; count--){
                    console.log("Current Count : " + count );
                }
                console.log("Loop stopped!");
        </script>
    </body>
</html>
```

This example displays the reverse loop count. It first initializes the count value as 10. The condition checks that the value of count is greater than 0. At every loop pass, the value of count is decremented by 1. The output of this program is shown in Figure 4-13.

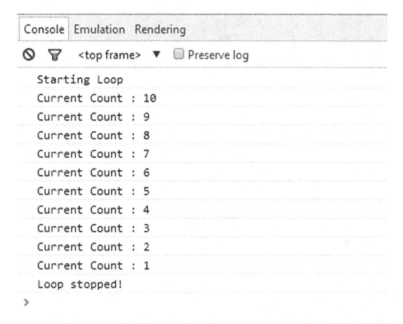

Figure 4-13. Program output

As you can see, the first value printed is 10 because the initial value of count is 10. The code within the loop is run as long as the value of count is greater than 0 (so the last value printed is 1).

Within the for loop code block, you can also include an if structure. Suppose you have the requirement to print all the even numbers from 0 to 19. You can achieve that by using a combination of a for loop and an if statement, as shown in Listing 4-10.

Listing 4-10. for Loop with if Statement

```
<html>
    <body>
        <script>
            var i;
            for(i = 0; i < 20; i++)
            {
                if((i % 2) == 0)
                {
                console.log("Number is divisible by 2 : " + i );
                continue;
                }
            }
        </script>
    </body>
</html>
```

This example uses the if statement in the for loop to check whether variable i is divisible by 2. In each case in which the value of i is divisible by 2, the program prints the value. The output of the program is shown in Figure 4-14.

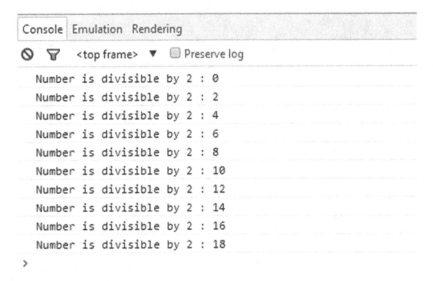

Figure 4-14. *Program output*

You may also nest a for loop, meaning you may have a for loop within a for loop. You will see an example of this in conjunction with the label keyword after the discussion of the for...in loop.

■ **Note**   The break statement may be used inside for loops as well, to exit the loop.

---

for...in Loop

The for...in loop is a special type of a loop that is run on the properties of an object. The for...in loop iterates a specified variable on all the properties of an object in question.

The for...in syntax is

```
for (variable in object) {
  statements
}
```

Listing 4-11 provides an example of the for...in loop being used in a program.

Listing 4-11. for...in Example

```
<html>
  <body>
    <script>
      var obj = {a:"alto", b:"scorpio", c:"zen"};
      for(var string=" " in obj) {
          console.log(obj[string]);
      }
    </script>
  </body>
</html>
```

Listing 4-11 introduces an object obj with three properties a, b, and c that are assigned values alto, scorpio, and zen, respectively. The for...in obj loop is then used to process each property of the object. In each iteration, one property from object is assigned to variable name and the loop continues until all the properties of object have been read. The console.log method is used to display the property content on the web browser console.

The output of the program is shown in Figure 4-15.

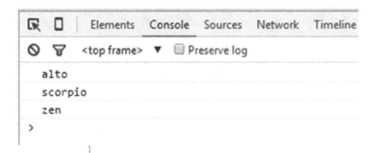

Figure 4-15. *Properties of object printed*

Label Statement

The label statement enables you to define a unique identifier for a statement block. The syntax is

```
label:
    statements
```

The name of the label is followed by a colon, and below the label is the block of statements linked with the label name (or defined by the given label). To clarify, consider the example in Listing 4-12.

Listing 4-12. Label Example

```html
<html>
    <body>
        <script>
            var i, j;
          Outerloop:
              for (i = 0; i < 5; i++) {
              for (j = 0; j < 5; j++) {
                    if (i === 1 && j === 1) {
                            break Outerloop;
                }
            }
            console.log("i = " + i + ", j = " + j);
        }
    }
        </script>

    </body>
</html>
```

Listing 4-12 defines a label Outerloop for the outer for loop. There is also an inner loop run for each iteration of the outer loop. To exit the outer loop when the values of counters i and j are both equal to 1, the break statement is used with the previously defined label Outerloop to denote the outer for loop. The output of Listing 4-12 is shown in Figure 4-16.

Figure 4-16. *Program output*

Summary

This chapter covered the various control structures in the JS language and described how to use them to fulfill requirements. It started with the block statements supported in JavaScript. Next, it covered the if...else and switch statements. Finally, demo programs showed you how to execute the various types of loops supported in JavaScript, including the for and while loops, along with the LABEL statement.

Chapter 5 discusses another important topic in JavaScript: regular expressions and string methods.

CHAPTER 5

■ ■ ■

Regular Expressions and String Methods

This chapter introduces you to an important feature of JS: regular expression processing. You use this feature to find and replace text matching a given pattern within a given text stream. The chapter first explains regular expressions as defined in JavaScript. It then shows you how to use RegExp in conjunction with string methods. The latter half of the chapter introduces you to the properties and methods of the RegExp object.

Regular Expressions: An Overview

Regular expressions consist of patterns (along with optional modifiers) used to match character combinations in a text string. Regular expressions provide a way to perform all types of string search and replacements. There are two ways to define regular expression objects in JavaScript. The first is shown here:

```
var pattern = new RegExp(pattern, attributes);
```

The other way is shown here:

```
var pattern = /pattern/attributes or modifiers;
```

It consists of a pattern and one or more optional flags (i.e., modifiers or attributes). The pattern indicates the regular expression pattern to be matched, whereas the attributes or modifiers specify any additional information. As the name indicates, modifiers are used to modify the search of the pattern within the text in question. The values that may be specified as attributes are

- g: Global modifier. Searches for all occurrences of a given pattern within a string.

- i: Ignores the case-sensitive behavior within a pattern search.

- m: Multiline modifier. Any ^ or $ specified in the regular expression applies to every line of the string. Without this modifier, it is applicable only once to the entire string.

Within the regular expression patterns, there are metacharacters and quantifiers. *Metacharacters* are special-meaning characters used for defining search patterns. Some of the commonly used metacharacters are shown in Table 5-1. There can be several occurrences of substrings identified by the metacharacters in the text string to be processed.

Table 5-1. *Metacharacters*

Metacharacter	Purpose
.	Searches for a character
\s	Searches for a blank character
\S	Searches for a non-whitespace character
\w	Searches for an alphanumeric character such as 1, 2, a, A, h, d, etc. (i.e., a word character, meaning a character from a-z, A-Z, or 0-9, and includes the underscore character, _)
\W	Searches for a nonalphanumeric character such as %, #, % (i.e., a non-word character)
\d	Searches for a digit such as 1, 2, or 3.
\D	Searches for a nondigit character such as *, #, a, b.

Quantifiers are used to specify the number of occurrences of a particular character or set of characters. Some of the commonly used quantifiers are shown in Table 5-2.

Table 5-2. *Quantifiers*

Quantifier	Purpose
p+	Matches occurrences of at least one *p*.
p*	Matches zero or more occurrences of *p*.
p?	Checks if a string contains zero or one occurrences of *p*.
p{A}	Matches a sequence of A number of *p*. For example, ab{2} will match abab.
p{A,B}	Checks if a string has a sequence of A to B number of *p*.
p{A,}	Checks if a string has a sequence of at least A number of *p*. For example, ab{1,} will match ab, abab, and so on.
p$	Matches a string that ends with *p*. For example, b$ will match ab, b, and cab.
^p	Matches a string that starts with *p*. For example, ^a will match ab, ah, and aj.

You can use square brackets in the regex pattern to specify which characters to search for. The typical uses of square brackets in expressions are shown in Table 5-3.

Table 5-3. *Usage of Square Brackets in Expressions*

Expression	Purpose
[xyz]	Searches for any character shown in the square brackets
[^xyz]	Searches for any character other than the ones in the brackets
[A-B]	Searches for a digit falling in the range A to B
[^A-B]	Finds any digit other than those falling in range A to B
(a|b)	Serves like an OR, searching for character a or b

■ **Note**   A detailed explanation of how to write regular expressions is beyond the scope of this chapter. However, we will focus on the JS methods that allow you to program regular expressions in order to solve typical user requirements.

There are two ways to use regular expressions:

- Use the String object methods
- Use the properties and methods of the regular expression objects (RegExp object)

Each is covered in turn in the following sections. Here are some examples of regular expressions:

```
var regex = /High/i ;
var regex = /[C-G]/gi ;
var re = /\s*;\s*/;
var text = new RegExp("Good morning", "g");
```

String Methods

In JavaScript, the following are the string methods pertaining to regular expression processing:

- search
- replace
- match
- split

Each of these string methods is covered in turn next, along with examples.

search Method

The search method uses an expression to search for a match, and returns the position of the match. The syntax for the search() method is

```
str.search(regexp)
```

The return value will be the index of the first match. A simple example of this is shown in Listing 5-1.

Listing 5-1. search() Method Example

```
<html>
    <body>
        <script>
            var text = "Visit the Google";
            console.log(text.search("Google"));
        </script>
    </body>
</html>
```

Listing 5-1 declares the variable text with some text ("Visit the Google"). The text.search() method searches for "Google" in variable text and returns its given position. The console.log() method is used to display the output.

The output for Listing 5-1 is shown in Figure 5-1.

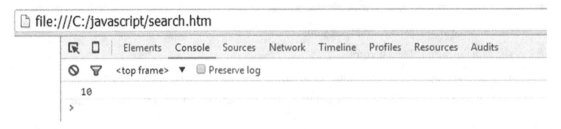

Figure 5-1. *Program output*

replace Method

As the name indicates, the replace method replaces a substring matching a given regular expression pattern within a text with another (new) substring. The modified string is then returned. The syntax for the replace() method is

```
str.replace(regexp, newsubstr)
```

The return value will be the new string with one or more matches of the given pattern replaced accordingly. Consider the example in Listing 5-2.

Listing 5-2. replace() Method Example

```
<html>
   <body>
      <script>
         var text = "High level language";
         console.log(text.replace(/High/i, "Low"));
      </script>
   </body>
</html>
```

In Listing 5-2, the text.replace() method is used to replace the string "High" with "Low". Modifier i is used to ignore the case.

The output of Listing 5-2 is shown in Figure 5-2.

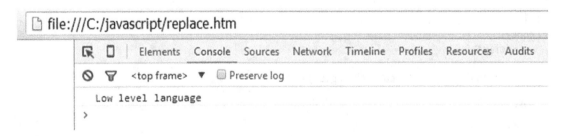

Figure 5-2. *Output*

■ **Note**   It is also possible to specify subgroups within the pattern to be matched. With the `replace` method, these subgroups may be addressed using placeholders `$1` and `$2`. For example:

```
var regex = /(\d+)\s(\d+)/;
var string1 = "123 321";   var newstring = string1.replace(regex, "$2, $1");
```

match Method

The `match` method is used to get all the substrings (regex matches) within a given text string in the form of an array. The usage of this method returns null if no match is found. The syntax for the `match()` method is

```
str.match(regexp)
```

Listing 5-3 shows an example of how the `match` method works.

Listing 5-3. match() Method Example

```
<html>
    <body>
        <script>
            var text = "Advance varsion of JavaScript 7.1.4";
            var result = text.match(/va/g);
            console.log(result);
        </script>
    </body>
</html>
```

This example declares the variable `text` with a string value. The `text.match()` method is then used to match the characters 'va' against the string value. The output for Listing 5-3 is shown in Figure 5-3.

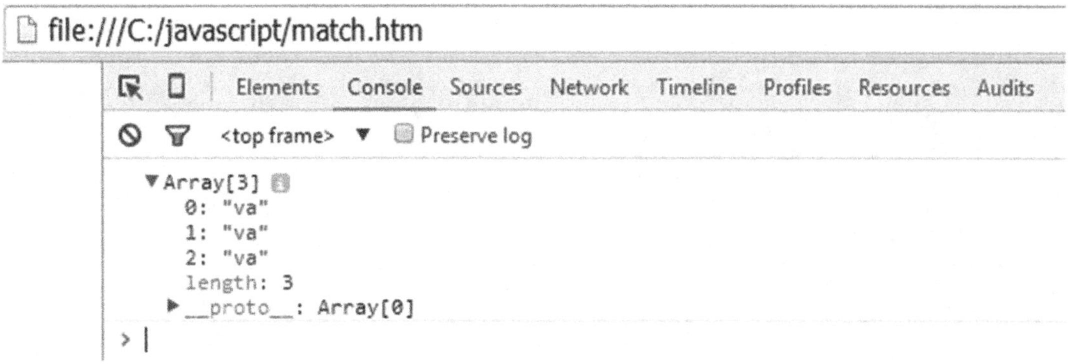

Figure 5-3. *Output*

69

Another example of the match method is shown in Listing 5-4.

Listing 5-4. Another match() Method Example

```html
<html>
  <body>
    <script>
      var text = "ABCDEFG12345abcdefghijklm";
      var result = text.match(/[C-G]/gi)
      console.log(result);
    </script>
  </body>
</html>
```

The example demonstrates the use of global (g) and ignore (i) case modifiers/flags with the match() method. It declares the variable text and assigns a text value to it. The text.match() method is used to find all the letters from C to G and/or c to g. the results are then returned in the array result.

The output of Listing 5-4 is shown in Figure 5-4.

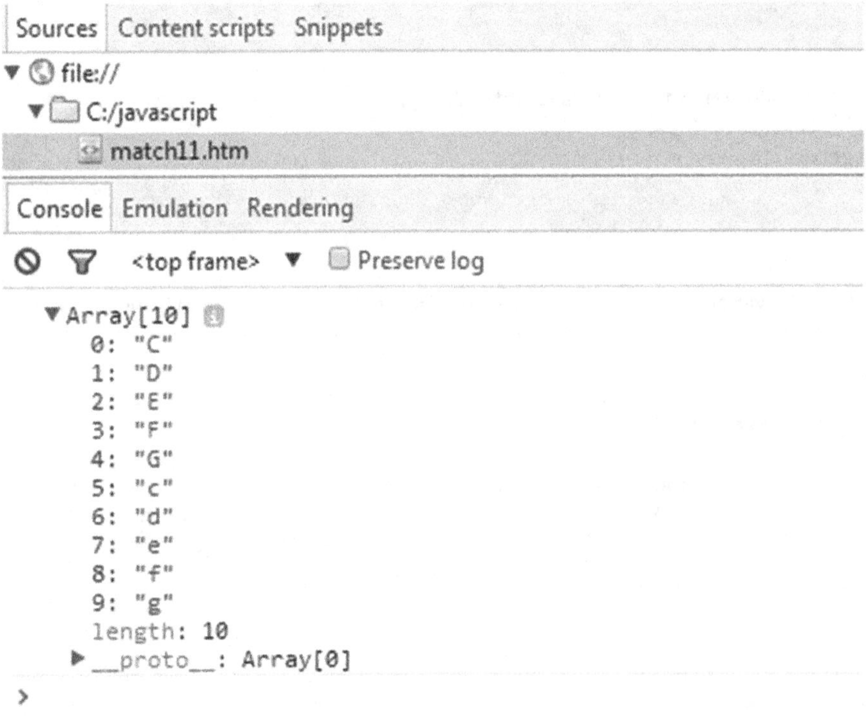

| Sources | Content scripts | Snippets |

▼ ⊙ file://
  ▼ 🗀 C:/javascript
      ⬘ match11.htm

| Console | Emulation | Rendering |

⊘ ▽   <top frame> ▼   ☐ Preserve log

```
▼ Array[10] 🔢
    0: "C"
    1: "D"
    2: "E"
    3: "F"
    4: "G"
    5: "c"
    6: "d"
    7: "e"
    8: "f"
    9: "g"
    length: 10
  ▶ __proto__: Array[0]
>
```

Figure 5-4. *Output*

split Method

In the context of regular expressions, the split method is used to split a string into an array of substrings that match a given regex pattern. The syntax of the split method is

```
str.split(regex, Limit)
```

If used without regular expressions, you may specify the separator in place of the regex. The syntax will then look like

```
str.split(separator, limit)
```

As mentioned earlier, the return value will be in the form of an array. The limit is a number (for example, 2, 10, etc.) that specifies the maximum number of elements contained in the result array. Both the separator and limit (integers) are optional.

An example of using the split method to remove spaces from a string is shown in Listing 5-5.

Listing 5-5. split Method Example

```
<html>
<body>
    <script>
      var countries = "UK ; US; Europe;  India";
      console.log(countries);
      var re = /\s*;\s*/;
      var countriesList = countries.split(re);
      console.log(countriesList);
    </script>
  </body>
</html>
```

This example declares the variable countries and assigns it a number of country names separated by a semicolon (;) contained within spaces. As you can see, the regular expression pattern used in the split method looks for zero or more spaces followed by a semicolon, then again followed by zero or more spaces. When such a pattern is found within the variable countries, a split is performed and the spaces and the semicolon are removed from the resulting substring. For each match, the array element is populated. The countriesList is the array returned as a result of split.

The output of Listing 5-5 is shown in Figure 5-5, displaying the original string and also the resulting array.

Figure 5-5. *Output*

Another usage of the split method using the optional limited number of splits is shown in Listing 5-6.

Listing 5-6. Another split() Method Example

```html
<html>
  <body>
    <script>
      var myString = 'Hello, this is JavaScript coding';
      var splits = myString.split(' ', 1);
      console.log(splits);
    </script>
  </body>
</html>
```

In this example, split will look for space in the string myString and stop when the first match is found. The output of Listing 5-6 is shown in Figure 5-6.

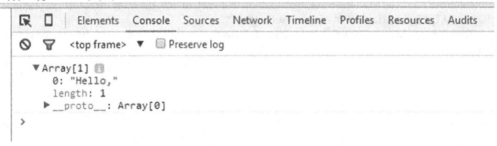

Figure 5-6. *Program output*

Regular Expression Object

Now that you are familiar with the basics of the regular expression object, this section dives into the details of its various properties and methods.

Regular Expression Object Properties

Table 5-4 shows the properties of the regular expression object.

Table 5-4. *Regular Expression Object Properties*

Property	Description
constructor	Contains the function that creates the object's prototype.
global	Specifies whether the g modifier is set for the given regular expression.
ignoreCase	Specifies whether the i modifier is set for the given regular expression.
lastIndex	Specifies the index at which to start the next match.
multiline	Specifies whether the m modifier is set for the given regular expression.
source	Represents the text of the pattern that is to be searched.

constructor Property

The constructor property contains the reference to the function that created the object instance. The syntax of constructor usage is

```
RegExp.constructor
```

For regular expressions, the constructor property returns function RegExp() { [native code] }.

■ **Note**   The constructor property is applicable for other objects such as numbers and strings. For numbers, the constructor property returns function Number() { [native code] }. For strings, it returns function String() { [native code] }.

Listing 5-7 provides an example of how the constructor property works.

Listing 5-7. constructor Property Example

```html
<html>
    <body>
        <script>
                var text = new RegExp("Good morning", "g");
                console.log("text.constructor is:" + text.constructor);
        </script>
    </body>
</html>
```

The output of Listing 5-7 is shown in Figure 5-7.

Figure 5-7. *Program output*

Listing 5-8 shows another constructor property example.

Listing 5-8. constructor Property Example

```
<html>
   <body>
     <script>
              var num = new Number(6);
              console.log("num.constructor is:" + num.constructor);
     </script>
   </body>
</html>
```

The output for Listing 5-8 is shown in Figure 5-8.

🗋 file:///C:/javascript/constructor.htm

```
⌖  ☐  │  Elements  Console  Sources  Network  Timeline  Profiles  Resources  Audits

◯  ▽   <top frame>  ▼  ☐ Preserve log

  num.constructor is:function Number() { [native code] }
> │
```

Figure 5-8. *Program output*

global Property

The global property specifies whether the regular expression uses the global modifier (i.e., whether the g modifier is set or not). The syntax for accessing the global property is

RegExp.global

This property returns true if the g modifier is set, and returns false otherwise. See Listing 5-9 for an example.

Listing 5-9. global Property Example

```
<html>
   <body>
     <script>
              var text = "Learn JavaScript";
```

```
                var pattern1 = /Java/g;
                 var result = pattern1.global;
                console.log("Text is matched with Java:" + pattern1.global);
                 var pattern2 = /Java/
                  console.log("Text is matched with Java:" + pattern2.global);
        </script>
    </body>
</html>
```

The output for Listing 5-9 is shown in Figure 5-9.

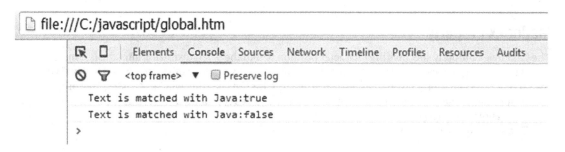

Figure 5-9. *Output*

ignoreCase Property

The ignoreCase property specifies whether the regular expression performs case-insensitive matching (in other words, whether the i modifier is set or not). The syntax to access this property is

RegExp.ignoreCase

The ignoreCase property returns true if the i modifier is set, and false otherwise.
Listing 5-10 presents a simple example of the usage of the ignoreCase property.

Listing 5-10. ignoreCase Property Example

```
<html>
    <body>
        <script>

                var pattern1 = /Java/i;
                console.log("IgnoreCase property is set:" + pattern1.ignoreCase);
                var pattern2 = /Java/;
                console.log("IgnoreCase property is set:" + pattern2.ignoreCase);
        </script>
    </body>
</html>
```

This example first declares regular expression pattern pattern1. In this case, the i modifier is specified, making it ignore the case. Next, the example declares pattern2 /Java/ without the ignoreCase modifier. In both cases, the output using the console.log method is generated for the ignoreCase property, as shown in Figure 5-10.

file:///C:/javascript/ignorecase.htm

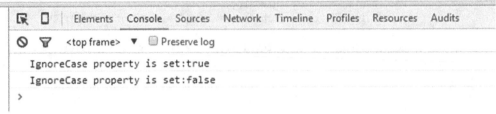

Figure 5-10. *Output*

lastIndex Property

The lastIndex property specifies the character position within the given text string after the last match found by the RegExp.exec() and RegExp.test() methods. For example, if the match found is "Java" where the second "a" is at the 14th position in the text string, the lastIndex value will be set as 15. This property is only applicable when the g modifier is set. The exec() and test() methods reset this property to 0 if no match (or another match) is found.

The syntax of lastIndex is

RegExp.ignoreCase

An example of the lastIndex property is shown in Listing 5-11.

Listing 5-11. lastIndex Property Example

```html
<html>
  <body>
    <script>
            var text = "We can use JavaScript in Java coding";

            var pattern = /Java/g;

            var result = pattern.test(text);
            console.log("Current index:" + pattern.lastIndex);

            var result = pattern.test(text);
            console.log("Current index:" + pattern.lastIndex);
    </script>
  </body>
</html>
```

This example has a text string and a regular expression using the global modifier. It uses the test method twice, each time followed by the display of the lastIndex property. The output for Listing 5-11 is shown in Figure 5-11.

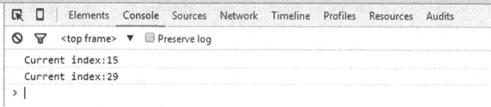

file:///C:/javascript/lastindex.htm

Current index:15
Current index:29

Figure 5-11. *Output*

multiline Property

The multiline property specifies whether the regular expression performs multiline matching. It checks whether the m modifier is set or not. The syntax of multiline is

RegExp.multiline

The property returns true if the m modifier is set, and returns false otherwise. Listing 5-12 presents an example of the multiline property.

Listing 5-12. multiline Property Example

```
<html>
    <body>
        <script>
                var text = "Learn JavaScript";
                var pattern1 = /Java/m;
                var result = pattern1.multiline;
                console.log("Text is matched with Java:" + pattern1.multiline);
                var pattern2 = /Java/;
                console.log("Text is matched with Java:" + pattern2.multiline);
        </script>
    </body>
</html>
```

The output of Listing 15-12 is shown in Figure 5-12.

file:///C:/javascript/multiline.htm

Text is matched with Java:true
Text is matched with Java:false

Figure 5-12. *Output*

source Property

The source property contains the text of the RegExp pattern. The syntax of the source property is

```
RegExp.source
```

As the name indicates, the source property returns the text used for pattern matching. It does not return the modifier, if any, used in the regular expression. Listing 5-13 shows an example of the source property.

Listing 5-13. source Property Example

```
<html>
    <body>
        <script>

            var pattern1 = /Java/g;
            console.log("Any text you have can be matched with the pattern:" + pattern1.source);
        </script>
    </body>
</html>
```

First a regex pattern1 is specified. The output of Listing 5-13 is shown in Figure 5-13.

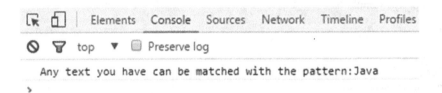

Figure 5-13. Output

Regular Expression Object Methods

There are four methods provided by the RegExp object, as listed and described in Table 5-5.

Table 5-5. Regular Expression Object Methods

Method	Description
exec()	Performs a search for a given regex pattern match within the parameter string
test()	Similar to exec but returns true when a match is found and false otherwise
toSource()	Returns an object literal representing the specified object
toString()	Returns a string representing the specified object

exec Method

The exec method searches a string for text that matches RegExp. The generic syntax of exec method is

```
RegExp.exec(string)
```

The `string` parameter denotes the string that is to be searched. The method returns the matched text (substring corresponding to the given Regex) if a match is found. Otherwise, `null` is returned. See Listing 5-14 for an example.

Listing 5-14. exec() Method Example

```html
<html>
    <body>
        <script>
                var text = "Learn JavaScript its very interesting script";

                var pattern = new RegExp( "Java", "g" );
                var result = pattern.exec(text);
                console.log("Text is matched with Java:" + result);

                var pattern1 = new RegExp( "language", "g" );
                    result = pattern1.exec(text);
                console.log("Text is matched with language:" + result);
        </script>
    </body>
</html>
```

This example first declares a `text` variable and assigns a string that is to be searched. Two patterns, `pattern1` and `pattern2`, are declared using the new keyword and built-in RegExp object. For both the variables `pattern1` and `pattern2`, the method exec is called using the same "text" string. The result is then returned in variable `result`.

The output of Listing 15-14 is shown in Figure 5-14.

file:///C:/javascript/exec.htm

Elements Console Sources Network Timeline Profiles Resources Audits

○ ▽ <top frame> ▼ ☐ Preserve log

```
Text is matched with Java:Java
Text is matched with language:null
>  |
```

Figure 5-14. *Output*

test Method

The test method also searches the given string for text that matches the regular expression pattern. If a match is found, it returns true. Otherwise, it returns false. The syntax of test() is

```
RegExp.test( string )
```

The test method takes as input a string parameter, as shown in Listing 5-15.

Listing 5-15. test Method Example

```
<html>
   <body>
      <script>
               var text = "Learn JavaScript its very interesting script";

               var pattern = new RegExp( "Java", "g" );
               var result = pattern.test(text);
               console.log("Text is matched with Java:" + result);

               var pattern = new RegExp( "language", "g" );
               var result = pattern.test(text);
               console.log("Text is matched with language:" + result);
      </script>
   </body>
</html>
```

The output of Listing 15-5 is shown in Figure 5-15.

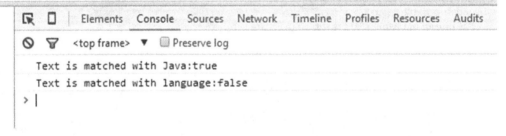

file:///C:/javascript/test.htm

```
Text is matched with Java:true
Text is matched with language:false
```

Figure 5-15. *Output*

toString Method

The toString method returns the corresponding string representation of a regular expression in the form of a regex literal. The returned string is contained within backslashes and also includes the modifiers, if applicable. The syntax of toString() is

```
RegExp.toString(string )
```

Listing 15-16 presents an example of the toString method in action.

Listing 5-16. toString() Method Example

```
<html>
    <body>
        <script>
                var text ;
                var pattern = new RegExp( "Java", "g" );
                var result = pattern.toString(text);
                console.log("Return value:" + result);

                var pattern = new RegExp( "/", "g" );
                var result = pattern.toString(text);
                console.log("Return value:" + result);
        </script>
    </body>
</html>
```

This example specifies two patterns via the RegExp object and then calls the toString method for both of the patterns. The output of Listing 5-16 is shown in Figure 5-16.

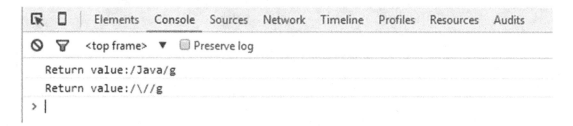

Figure 5-16. *Output*

■ **Note**   The exec and test methods are similar to the extent that both take as input the string that is to be searched. The difference is that exec returns the matched substring or null value, whereas the test method returns true or false.

Summary

This chapter introduced you to regular expressions, including how to use RegExp in conjunction with string methods. You were also exposed to the properties and methods of the RegExp object, along with code examples.

Chapter 6 discusses another important topic in JavaScript: functions.

CHAPTER 6

Functions

This chapter introduces you to the basics of functions and the advantages that they provide. First, you will be shown the different types of methods used for creating functions in JavaScript. Then, you will see how to define functions that return values to the calling program as well as how to specify parameters (arguments) for the defined function.

Functions: An Overview

A *function* may be simply defined as a set of statements or a subprogram that can be used or called anywhere within the JS program. A function typically has a name, but does not have to have a name, in which case it is called an *anonymous function*. A function can have zero or more parameters.

A function has a body that is enclosed within curly brackets, and the body of the function may include several statements. A function may also include a `return` statement, which is optional and may be used to return to the caller code a computed value. (You'll learn more about the `return` statement later in this chapter.) The processing of the function stops at the `return` statement.

Using function provides the following advantages to developers:

- It saves a lot of time and effort because the developer doesn't need to rewrite the code for a particular requirement.

- The code of the program is more compact, more organized, and more understandable than it would be without functions.

- After functions are defined once, they may be used throughout the program or in other functions.

To define functions in JavaScript, you use the `function` keyword, followed by a unique function name, a parameters list, and a block of code in curly brackets. The syntax of a function is

```
function name(parameter-list)
    {
        statements
    }
```

Here, `name` is the function name, `parameter-list` represents the list of arguments to be passed to the function, and `statements` include the body of the function and may or may not include calls to other functions.

If the function has no parameters, you still need to include the parentheses after the function name:

```
function name()
    {
        statements
    }
```

For simplicity sake, this chapter only shows functions that have a name.

The example in Listing 6-1 shows the named function and how the value is returned from a function.

Listing 6-1. Function Example

```
function triple(num){
    return ( 3  * num );
}
```

This simple example triples the number num. The name of the function is triple and num is the parameter whose tripled value is to be calculated. The computed value is then returned.

This function may be used in a console.log method, or in an alert function as follows:

```
alert( 'Tripled figure is '+ triple(2));
```

The output of this code is shown in Figure 6-1.

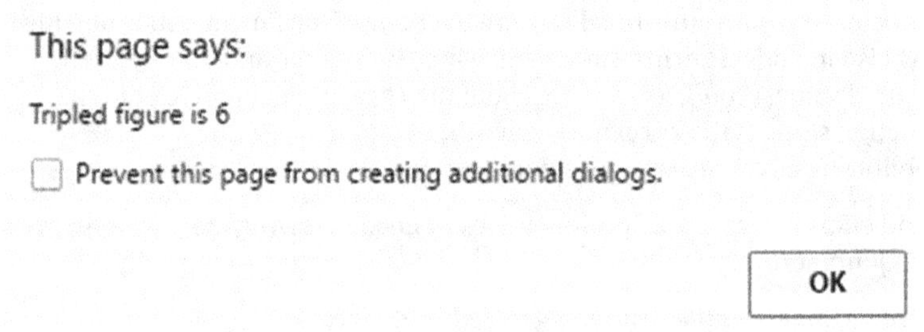

This page says:

Tripled figure is 6

☐ Prevent this page from creating additional dialogs.

OK

Figure 6-1. *Output*

As previously mentioned, to invoke the function correctly, you need to use the function ( ) operator. Omitting the operator ( ) leads to the code of the function (definition) being returned. Consider the example shown in Figure 6-2.

Listing 6-2. Omitted Function Operator Example

```
alert( 'Tripled figure is '+ triple);
```

The output of Listing 6-2 is shown in Figure 6-2.

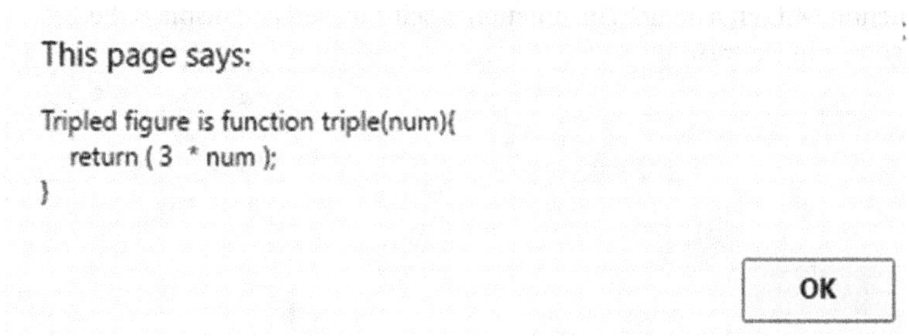

This page says:

Tripled figure is function triple(num){
    return (3 * num);
}

```
                                            OK
```

Figure 6-2. *Output*

Declaring Functions

Now that you are familiar with the basics of functions in JS, this section describes some of the ways that you can create functions in programs. Functions can be created mainly in two ways:

- Using a function expression
- Using a function declaration

The following subsections cover each and their further classification in detail.

Using a Function Expression

This option involves defining a function within a larger expression. A function defined via a function expression can be any of three types:

- Self-invoking functions
- Named function expression
- Anonymous function expression

Self-Invoking Functions

A self-invoking function is a function that may be defined with a name or without a name but is invoked automatically. There is no declaration and invocation involved. The expression executes the function automatically.

The syntax for a self-invoking function is shown here:

```
(function(){
// code
})();
```

Again, it is absolutely essential that the function name is followed by parentheses, ().
Listing 6-3 shows a working example of a self-invoking function.

Listing 6-3. Self-Invoking Function Example

```
(function () {
    console.log("See you all!");
})();
```

This example declares the function without a name. The function is self-invoked and displays the output in the browser console, as shown in Figure 6-3.

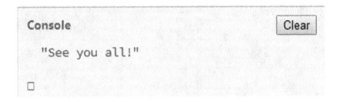

Figure 6-3. *Output*

Named Function Expression

As the name suggests, the named function is declared with a name in a function expression.

The syntax of a named function is

```
var myFunction = function namedFunction(){
    statements
}
```

Here, a variable myFunction is defined, to which the function object is assigned. You may then use the variable myFunction and supply any values pertaining to the function, if applicable, in order to execute the code of the function.

Consider the example in Listing 6-4, which declares the function name as myFunction and assigns it to the declared variable myValue.

Listing 6-4. Named Functions Example

```
var myValue = function myFunction() {
        return 'Hello';
    }
console.log("Text displayed as : " +myValue());
```

The output of Listing 6-4 is shown in Figure 6-4.

Console   Clear

"Text displayed as : Hello"

Figure 6-4. *Output*

Anonymous Function

A function (expression) that does not have a name is called an anonymous function. The syntax of an anonymous function is

```
var myFunction = function() {
    statements
}
```

Listing 6-5 shows an example of an anonymous function.

Listing 6-5. Anonymous Function Example

```
var myFunction = function()
    {
        return 'Hello';
    }
console.log("Text displayed as : " +myFunction());
```

This example assigns the result of the function expression in question to a variable myFunction and calls it using myFunction.

The output of Listing 6-5 is shown in Figure 6-5.

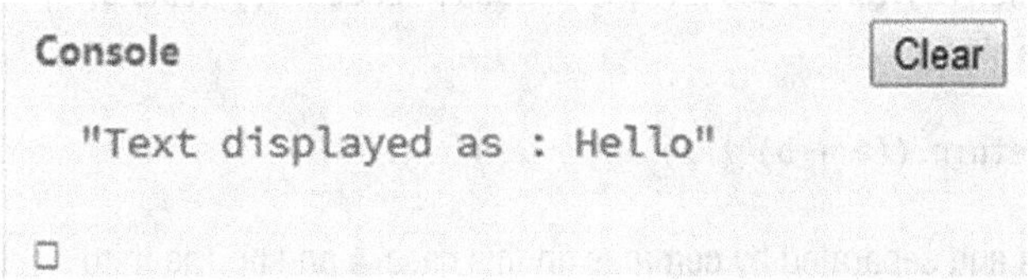

Figure 6-5. *Output*

Using a Function Declaration

A function declaration defines a function with a name and does not involve any variable assignment. Declared functions are only executed when called and are not executed immediately.

The syntax of a function declaration is

```
function funct_name(parameters) {
    Statements
}
```

Listing 6-6 shows an example of a function declaration.

Listing 6-6. Function Declaration Example

```
function myFunction()
    {
        return 'Hello';
    }
console.log("Text displayed as : " +myFunction());
```

In the example, myFunction() is the declared function and is called within the console.log function. It returns the value "Hello" whenever it is called in the program.

■ **Note**   A function declaration is not an executable statement. It is not necessary to have a semicolon at the end of a function declaration.

The output of Listing 6-6 is shown in Figure 6-6.

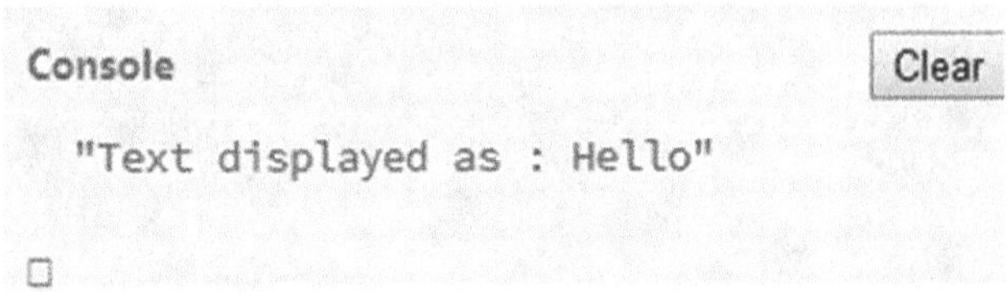

Figure 6-6. *Output*

■ **Note**   In addition to the function expression and function declaration, there is also a function constructor way of creating functions. In this approach, the new keyword is used. The constructor Function() treats the code as stored in strings. One example of this is shown:

```
var average = new Function('a', 'b', 'return ((a + b) / 2)' );
```

Here, the parameters are supplied within quotes and separated by commas (in this case, a and b). The third string is the code. This method is slow and difficult to debug and therefore not recommended.

It is better to use a function expression or a function declaration.

Summary Comparison of the Function Declaration and Function Expression

This is a declaration:

```
function product(a, b) {
    return a * b;
}
```

This is an expression:

```
var product = function (a, b) {
    return a * b;
};
```

Function Parameters and Arguments

As mentioned earlier in this chapter, a function may or may not include parameters. There may be one or more parameters for a given function.

Based on the parameter values supplied to the function, the behavior of the function changes and results compute accordingly. Parameters such as a and b may be addressed like any local variables within the code of the function. These parameters are specified within parentheses, separated by commas.

In the following example, p1 and p2 are parameters:

```
function anexample(p1, p2) {
    ...
}
```

At the time of the function invocation, the corresponding values supplied for the parameters are known as *arguments*. In the following example, 10 and 11 are arguments:

```
anexample(10,11);
```

An example of in Listing 6-7.

Listing 6-7. Function Parameter Example

```
<!DOCTYPE html>
<html>
    <body>
        <script>
            function mymessage(user) {
            console.log("Good to see you " + user);
            }
            mymessage("Diego Dora")
        </script>
    </body>
</html>
```

In this code, function mymessage uses one parameter, user, at the time of declaration. It takes a string of text as a parameter. Next, function mymessage is called and passed the text "Diego Dora".

The output of Listing 6-7 is shown in Figure 6-7.

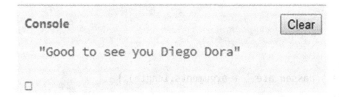

Figure 6-7. *Output*

Missing Parameters and the undefined Value

It is possible to invoke a multiparameter function and omit a few of the parameters. Within the function, any missing parameters have the value set as undefined. Any extra arguments supplied are ignored.

Consider the code in Listing 6-8.

Listing 6-8. Missing Parameter Example

```
function myFunction(firstparam, secondparam) {
    if (secondparam === undefined) {
        console.log(secondparam)
    }
}
myFunction(1);
```

Listing 6-8 is an example involving missing parameters. The function myFunction has two parameters, firstparam and secondparam. Within the code, the if statement checks whether the value of secondparam is supplied, checking it against value undefined. The function is then called and only one argument is passed. In this case, because the value of secondparam has not been set, the function checks the if condition and displays undefined.

The output of Listing 6-8 is shown in Figure 6-8.

Figure 6-8. Output

arguments Array

A function may include a special array named arguments that contains all of the arguments supplied via the function call. This array contains a value even when no parameters are defined in the function definition. An example demonstrating the arguments array is shown in Listing 6-9.

Listing 6-9. arguments Array Example

```
function myFunction() {
        console.log(arguments[0]);
        console.log(arguments[1]);
        console.log('Total Parameters passed are ' + arguments.length) }
myFunction('Diego Dora' , 'Jon Reed');
```

This example has a function myFunction that has no parameters specified in the declaration. Within the function, the first and second elements of the array arguments are displayed, and also the total length of the array. The example then calls the function and supplies two arguments. The code does not produce any errors.

The output of Listing 6-9 is shown in Figure 6-9.

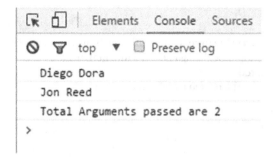

Diego Dora
Jon Reed
Total Arguments passed are 2

Figure 6-9. Output

Simulating Optional Parameter Passing

It is also possible to make parameters optional in functions. Listing 6-10 shows how it works.

Listing 6-10. Optional Argument Example

```
function myDivision(number, divisor) {
  if (divisor === undefined)
  {
      return('Division by zero not possible');
  }
  else

      return  number / divisor;
  }
console.log(myDivision(8));
console.log(myDivision(100, 10));
```

   The example shows division of numbers. The function myDivision can be called either with two arguments or with a single argument. Since no divisor is supplied in the first function call, in order to avoid division by zero, the value of divisor is checked, and the appropriate message is displayed. When the same function myDivision is called a second time, both the number and divisor are passes as 100 and 10, respectively. This time the division is performed and the value outputted.
   The output of Listing 6-10 is shown in Figure 6-10.

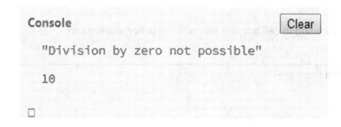

Figure 6-10. Output

return Statement

The return statement is required when/if you want to return a value from a function—that is, it returns a computed value to the function caller. A return statement should be the last one in a function, because the execution is stopped once the return statement is encountered.

Listing 6-11 shows an example of how the return statement works in a division operation.

Listing 6-11. return Statement Example

```html
<html>
<body>
<script>
        var result = function(number, divisor)
        {
          return number / divisor;
        };
        console.log(result(150, 10))
</script>
</body>
</html>
```

The function shown has two parameters, number and divisor. The return statement is used to return the value to the caller. At the time of execution, when the return statement is reached, the control is immediately given, along with the computed value, to the caller.

The output of Listing 6-11 is shown in Figure 6-11.

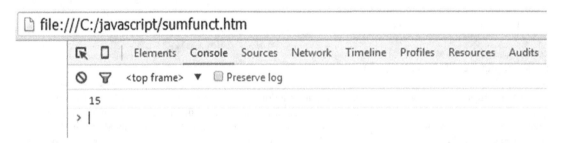

Figure 6-11. *Output*

Function Call

As mentioned earlier, it is also possible for a function to call another function. To better understand, consider the example in Listing 6-12.

Listing 6-12. Function Calling Other Function Example

```html
<!DOCTYPE html>
<html>
   <body>
      <script>
         function total1(a, b) {
               return a + b;
         }
         function  average(a, b) {
```

```
            var av = total1(a, b) / 2;

            console.log("Average = " + av);
        }
        average(8, 8);
    </script>
  </body>
</html>
```

This example calculates the average of two numbers. It declares two functions, total1 and average, both of which have two parameters, a and b. The total1 function returns the sum or total of the two numbers. Within the average function, the total1 function is called first to compute the total of the two numbers, and then this total is divided by 2 to calculate the average. The console.log function is used to display the average. The average function is called with values 8 and 8.

The output of Listing 6-12 is shown in Figure 6-12.

Figure 6-12. *Output*

Parameter Pass by Value or Pass by Reference?

In JavaScript, you cannot pass parameters by reference. When you pass a variable to a function, JS makes a copy of the parameter and works on it. Hence, within the function, the value of the parameter passed cannot be altered.

To better understand why you cannot pass parameters by reference, consider the example presented in Listing 6-13.

Listing 6-13. Pass by Reference Attempt Example

```
function decNumber(countVal) {
    countVal--;
}
var i = 10;
decNumber(i);
console.log("Value after attempt is : " + i);
```

The example shows an attempt to change the value of variable i using function decNumber. It declares the function decNumber and passes countVal. The value of variable i is not changed even after the call to function decNumber.

The output Listing 6-13 is shown in Figure 6-13.

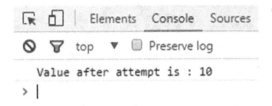

Figure 6-13. *Output*

An indirect way for JS to carry out a change of a value passed to the function is via the usage of arrays. The same example with the change is shown in Listing 6-14.

Listing 6-14. Pass by Value Function Example

```
function decNumber(countVal) {
    countVal[0]--;
}
var i = [10];
decNumber(i);
console.log("Value decremented to : " + i[0]);
```

The example shows how the value of the array element is decremented using function decNumber(). It declares an array i whose element 0 is assigned the value that is to be changed. This array is passed as an argument to the function. Within the function code, the zeroth element of the array is decremented by 1. Upon function execution, the value is changed and displayed.

The output of Listing 6-14 is shown in Figure 6-14.

Console   Clear

"Value decreamnet to : 9"

☐

Figure 6-14. *Output*

Function Naming

To wrap up this chapter on JavaScript functions, a word of caution is in order: Never name your function by the name function. This is strictly not allowed. Consider the following code:

```
function function(countVal) {
    countVal--;
}
```

In this case, the error shown in Figure 6-15 occurs.

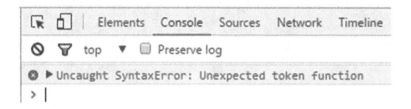

Figure 6-15. *Error*

Summary

In this chapter, you first explored the basics of functions and saw their advantages. You then saw how the functions are declared. With that important foundational knowledge in place, Chapter 7 will discuss advanced functions in JavaScript.

CHAPTER 7

■ ■ ■

Doing More with Functions

Chapter 6 introduced you to the basics of functions and how they make it easy to execute complex mathematical code. You learned how functions are created and how they perform a task every time you call and invoke them. You also saw different ways of using functions, parameters, and arguments. This chapter covers more advanced topics pertaining to functions. You will see how hoisting applies to functions, and learn why functions are called "first-class citizens." You will also learn how to declare nested functions, how to apply closures to functions, and how to declare recursive functions.

Hoisting in the Context of Functions

As mentioned in Chapter 1, *variable hoisting* means using a variable before it is actually declared. Hoisting is fully supported in the context of functions as well. This means that you can call a function even before it is declared.

Consider the example of function hoisting in Listing 7-1.

Listing 7-1. Function Hoisting

```
<html>
 <body>
  <script>
   say_hello_to_user();

   function say_hello_to_user(){
      alert('Hello how are you, today?');
   }
  </script>
 </body>
</html>
```

This code works perfectly and does not produce any syntax errors. The first line in the script is the call to the say_hello_to_user function. The declaration of this function actually comes later. JavaScript moves the declaration of the function to the start of the scope. This is equivalent to the example shown in Listing 7-2.

© Rehan Zaidi 2017

R. Zaidi, *JavaScript Essentials for SAP ABAP Developers*, DOI 10.1007/978-1-4842-2220-1_7

Listing 7-2. Equivalent JS Code

```
<script>

 function say_hello_to_user(){
    alert('Hello how are you, today?');
  }
 say_hello_to_user();
</script>
```

The output of both listings is shown in Figure 7-1.

This page says:

Hello how are you, today?

Figure 7-1. *Program output*

■ **Note** Variable declarations are not completely hoisted.

It is worth noting that if there is any syntax error in the function body or the code prior to the function code, the syntax of the function body is checked first and any syntax error is highlighted. This is shown in Figure 7-2.

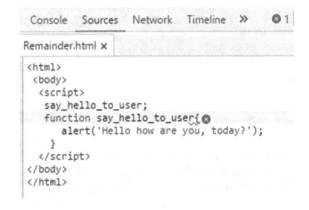

Figure 7-2. *Syntax error in function code*

Attempting to use a variable declaration along with a function expression results in a syntax error. Consider the example shown in Listing 7-3.

Listing 7-3. Example of Incorrect Code

```
<script>

hello();
var hello    = function say_hello_to_user(){
    alert('Hello how are you, today?');
  }

</script>
```

This code produces a syntax error, as shown in Figure 7-3.

```
<html>
  <body>
   <script>
    hello();  ⊗
    var hell\    = function say hello to user(){
        al ⊗ Uncaught TypeError: hello is not a function
      }

   </script>
```

Figure 7-3. Syntax error

Consider another example of incorrect code in Listing 7-4.

Listing 7-4. Second Incorrect Code Example

```
<script>

var hello;
hello();
hello    = function say_hello_to_user(){
    alert('Hello how are you, today?');
  }

</script>
```

This program also produces a syntax error. Here we try to a variable hello. The attempt to use the variable hello as a function is not acceptable to JS, and the syntax error results in program shown in Figure 7-4.

Figure 7-4. Syntax error

First-Class Citizens

Within JavaScript, functions are treated as first-class citizens. They may be

- Assigned to a variable

- Passed as a parameter to a function

- The returned value of a function

For purposes of comparison, Listing 7-5 shows a simple function example.

Listing 7-5. Simple Function Example

```
<!DOCTYPE html>
<html>
   <body>
      <script>
         var myMessage = function()
         {
         console.log("Good To See You....!");
         };
      myMessage();
      </script>
   </body>
</html>
```

In this simple function example, myMessage does not list any parameter names (i.e., the function is empty). To invoke the function later in the script, you simply write the name of that function, as shown in the code. This calls the message and displays the message.

The output of Listing 7-5 is shown in Figure 7-5.

Figure 7-5. *Output*

Listing 7-6 shows an example of how you can pass as input a function to another function and return it from the function itself.

Listing 7-6. First-Class Citizen Example

```
<html>
<body>
<script>

var function1 = function() {
  console.log("Function 1 Called");
};
```

```
var function2 = function(input) {
  return input;
};

function2(function1)();

</script>
</body>
</html>
```

Here, the function outputs Function 1 Called in the console of the browser. This function is assigned to the variable function1 via assignment. Next, another anonymous function takes as input a parameter by the name input and returns it. This function is assigned to the variable function2. Finally, function2 is called and passed function1 as a parameter. Because function2 returns any value passed to it as the returning value, the following two expressions are equal:

- function2(function1)

- function1

To call function1, you must include the parentheses, (), a shown. Otherwise, a syntax error results. The output of the program is shown in Figure 7-6.

Figure 7-6. *Program output*

Nested Functions

A nested function, also known as an inner function, is a function that is defined within another function. The function within which the inner function is enclosed is known as the outer function. The inner function may or may not have a return statement. Upon each call of the outer function, an instance of the nested function gets created.

Consider the example of nested functions presented in Listing 7-7.

Listing 7-7. Nested Functions Example

```
<html>
 <body>
  <script>

    function myfunction(d1, d2) {
      function doDivision(d1, d2) {
          return d1 / d2;
      }
```

101

```
        return doDivision(d1, d2);
        }

    var div = myfunction(4, 2);
    console.log(div);
 </script>
</body>
</html>
```

This example shows the division of two numbers. The main, outer function is named myfunction, inside of which is defined the doDivision function. This inner function is called by supplying values 4 and 2, and the value of this is stored in variable div, which is later displayed in the browser console. At the time of the call to the outer function myfunction, an instance of the inner function doDivision is created.

Also note that parameters d1 and d2 are specified for both functions. This is allowed in JavaScript and does not lead to any issues. The output of the program is shown in Figure 7-7.

Figure 7-7. *Program output*

When dealing with nested functions, it is important to note that the inner function has access to the main outer function's scope. In other words, the function doDivision may use the parameters and the variables of the outer function myfunction. In Listing 7-7, the d1 and d2 arguments of myfunction are supplied to the inner function doDivision as arguments d1 and d2, respectively. This is not necessary because doDivision may access d1 and d2 of the outer function myfunction. Listing 7-8 shows how the code in Listing 7-7 may be simplified by relying on the fact that doDivision can access d1 and d2 of myfunction.

Listing 7-8. Second Nested Functions Example

```
<html>
 <body>
  <script>
      function myfunction(d1, d2) {
        function doDivision() {
            return d1 / d2;
        }
        return doDivision();
     }
    var div = myfunction(4, 2);
    console.log(div);
  </script>
 </body>
</html>
```

This is a better form of the nested division example because it removes the redundant parameters from the doDivision function. Inside the doDivision body, Listing 7-8 returns the division value of d1 / d2 (parameters d1 and d2 supplied to myfunction).

The output of this program is shown in Figure 7-8 and is the same as the output shown previously.

Figure 7-8. *Program output*

It is also possible to declare the nested function anonymously. The example shown in Listing 7-9 attempts to solve the same division problem from the previous two listings, but in a bit different, and more complicated, manner.

Listing 7-9. Anonymous Nested Function Example

```
<html>
<body>
<script>
        function doDivision(d2) {
         return function(d1) {
         return d1/d2;
         };
        }

        var div = doDivision(2);
        console.log(div(6));
</script>
</body>
</html>
```

In this form of nested functions, the return statement is used twice. The inner function uses the parameter d2 of the outer function. In addition, the inner function returns a reference to a function that takes as input the number to be divided. The first return statement is used to call other function for d1 and the second return statement returns the result of the division d1/d2.

The output of Listing 7-9 is shown in Figure 7-9.

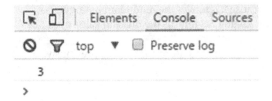

Figure 7-9. *Program output*

Let's take a look at yet another form of a nested function. It is also possible to call the inner function (declared within the outer function) within the body of the code of the outer function itself. Consider the example in Listing 7-10.

Listing 7-10. Calling the Inner Function

```
function myFunction() {
  var mytext = "Mytext";

  function showtext() {
      console.log(mytext);
  }
      showtext();
}
myFunction();
```

Here, the outer and inner functions are myFunction and showtext, respectively. A variable mytext is defined in myFunction. The inner function showtext is declared within myFunction. The showtext function is then called. When the function myFunction is called, the output in the console is as shown in Figure 7-10.

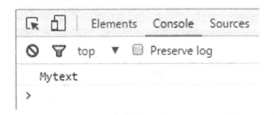

Figure 7-10. *Program output*

Lexical Scoping

In the context of functions, *lexical scoping* means that the scope of a variable is determined via the location of the variable within the JavaScript source code. Any variables that are declared outside of functions are accessible and visible to the entire JS program (i.e., global variables). On the other hand, variables declared within a given function are only visible and accessible to the code block of the function in question. This is called *function scope*. In the case of nested functions, the inner function has access to variables declared in the outer function. Any variable declared in the inner function may not be accessed outside of it.

Consider the example of lexical scoping in Listing 7-11.

Listing 7-11. Lexical Scoping Example

```
function myFunction() {
  var mytext = "Mytext";

  function showtext() {
      console.log(mytext);
  }

      showtext();
}
```

Function myFunction declares a local variable mytext and a function showtext—the inner function defined inside myFunction() that is available only in the body of myFunction. Here, showtext has no local variables, but it has access to those of its outer functions, in this case myFunction. Within the myFunction body, the showtext function is called in order to display the text contained in variable mytext.

Let's consider another example of lexical scoping in Listing 7-12.

Listing 7-12. Second Lexical Scoping Example

```
<html>
<body>
<script>
    var function1  = function(){
    var text1 = "Text1";
    function f2() {
            if(true){
                var text2  = "Text 2";
                console.log(text2);
            }

            if(true){
                console.log(text2);
            }
    }
    f2();
    console.log(text2) ; // gives error - ERROR
}
function1();

</script>
</body>
</html>
```

In this example, variable function1 is assigned to a function. Within this (outer) function is a variable text1 and an inner function f2. Within the inner function there are two if statements and two blocks (shown in curly brackets).

The variable text2 is accessible anywhere within the function f2, irrespective of the code block in which it is declared. However, text2 is not accessible outside the function f2. Hence, the error results with the last console.log statement. The text1 variable is accessible throughout the outer function.

Closures

Under normal circumstances, the local variables within a function only exist for the duration of that function's execution. After the function has executed, the local variables normally can't be accessed. However, it is possible to have local variables persist after the function's execution by using closure.

In JavaScript, you can create special functions known as *closures* that remember the environment (state) in which they were created. These include independent local variables within the function. So, in other words, a closure is composed of

- A function

- The environment of the function

Environment in this context means the local variables at the time of closure creation. Consider the non-closure example in Listing 7-13 that produces a syntax error.

Listing 7-13. Syntax Error

```
function myFunction() {
  var num = 10;
  }
 console.log(num);
```

This generates a syntax error because num is not accessible to the outside world. However, by using closure, num can be accessed. Consider the example in Listing 7-14.

Listing 7-14. Closure Example

```
function Func() {
  var num = 10;
  function returnnumber() {
    return num;
  }
  return returnnumber;
}

var closure1 = Func();
console.log(closure1());
```

When this code is executed, the output is as shown in Figure 7-11.

Figure 7-11. *Program output*

The number will be displayed in the console of the browser. The inner returnnumber function was returned from the outer function Func before execution. Func has become a closure. In this case, Func is a closure that contains both the function and the num value 10 that existed at the time of closure creation.

Listing 7-15 shows an example with a more useful purpose.

Listing 7-15. Division Using Closure

```
<html>
<body>
<script>

function divisionfactory(divisor) {
  return function performdivision(number) {
    return number / divisor ;
  }
}

var divideby10 = divisionfactory(10);
var divideby20 = divisionfactory(20);

console.log(divideby10(100));
console.log(divideby20(200));

</script>
</body>
</html>
```

This example defines a function `divisionfactory` that takes as input a parameter `divisor` and returns a reference to another function. The inner function is called `performdivision` (though you could have this as anonymous as well). The inner function has a single parameter, `number`, and returns the result of the division `number / divisor`. As the name suggests, the outer function `divisionfactory` is used to create functions that can be used to divide the inputted number with a specific value.

For the sake of the example, Listing 7-15 creates two functions, `divideby10` and `divideby20,` that divide their argument by 10 and 20, respectively. These two new functions are closures that have a similar body but separate environments. For `divideby20`, the value of `divisor` is 10, whereas in the case of `divideby10`, the value of division is 20.

The output of Listing 7-15 is shown in Figure 7-12.

Figure 7-12. *Division output*

Consider another interesting example of closure in Listing 7-16.

Listing 7-16. Another Closure Example

```
var add_element = (function() {
    var total_elements = 0;
    var array = [];
    return function addition(element) {
            array[total_elements] = element;
            console.log(array);
            total_elements = total_elements + 1;

 }
})();

add_element(10);
add_element(11);
add_element(12);
```

This example defines a function and assigns it to the variable add_element. Within the code, the variables total_elements and array are declared with initial values of 0 and [ ], respectively. The property element is assigned to the end of the array array. In addition, the total_elements counter is incremented by 1 upon each insertion of element to array. This function returns a function addition that adds a new element passed to it to the array and increments the count of elements in the array.

The example in Listing 7-16 calls add_element three times, supplying values 10, 11, and 12, respectively. The output of Listing 7-16 is shown in Figure 7-13.

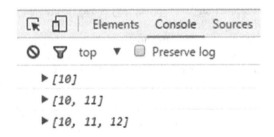

Figure 7-13. *Program output showing array elements*

The add_element is a closure that contains the function addition. However, because Listing 7-16 uses a self-invoking function, the initialization statements (setting array to [ ] and setting total_elements to 0) are executed only once. As you will see, each function closure remembers the state in which it was created. These include the variables array and total_elements.

Recursive Functions

As already mentioned in Chapter 6, it is possible for a function to call itself—that is, a function defined in terms of itself. Such functions are called *recursive functions*. Typical problems that may be solved using recursion include Fibonacci series problems and the famous Tower of Hanoi problem. Recursion provides some advantages to developers, such as the capability to develop neat and short code, and also helps developers to avoid loops.

When defining recursive functions, it is essential to specify a termination condition. If such a condition is not specified, an infinite "function" call may occur. In usual cases, a recursive function is declared as a named function. However, it is also possible to define an anonymous function as a recursive function.

Let's now take a look at a fully working example of a recursive function in JavaScript. Suppose we have the requirement to input a number and then spell each digit separately. For example, if the number 647 is passed as input, then the digits 6, 4, and 7 must be displayed separately, in the correct order.

The code pertaining to this example is shown in Listing 7-17.

Listing 7-17. Recursion Example

```
<html>
<body>
<script>
 function spell_number( num ) {
         if ( num < 10 ) {
            console.log(num);
          }
         else {
            spell_number( Math.floor(num / 10) ) ;
            console.log( num % 10 );
       }
   }
 spell_number(647);
</script>
</body>
</html>
```

The basic solution to the given problem is that a number to be spelled digit-wise is

- The number itself, if the number is less than 10

- The spelled digits of the quotient (obtained by division by 10), followed by the remainder of division by 10 of the number

Listing 7-17 declares a function by the name spell_number that takes as input a parameter num. Within the code, the function checks if the number supplied is less than 10. The terminating condition is when the number passed as input is less than 10. In this case, the function should return the number itself rather than calling the recursive function. The number is directly outputted to the console, and no recursive call to spell_number is made.

If the number is greater than or equal to 10, Listing 7-17 calls the function recursively and supplies it the quotient of num divided by 10. Next, the remainder of num divided by 10 is outputted in the console. Since we need to print the numbers in the correct order from left to right, we call the recursive function first and then print the remainder.

For the inputted number 647, the sequence of the call of function spell_number is as shown here:

- function spell_number(647)   function called with input 647

- function spell_number(64) // function called with input 64

- function spell_number(6)   function called with input 6

The output of the program is shown in Figure 7-14.

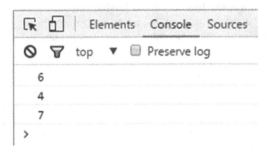

Figure 7-14. *Program output*

It is also possible to rewrite the same problem using an anonymous function in conjunction with a variable expression. Listing 7-18 shows how this may be done.

Listing 7-18. Anonymous Recursive Function

```
<html>
<body>
<script>
  var spell_number = function( num ) {
          if ( num < 10 ) {
              console.log(num);
           }
          else {
              spell_number( Math.floor( num / 10) ) ;
              console.log( num % 10 );
       }
    }
  spell_number(647);

</script>
</body>
</html>
```

As you can see, most of the code is the same as in Listing 7-17. The only difference is that Listing 7-18 defines the function without a name and specifies a variable spell_number to which the function declaration is assigned. The call to the recursive function is done via the variable spell_number. The output of the program is the same.

Summary

In this chapter, you first saw how hoisting is applied to functions, and then you discovered why functions are called first-class citizens. You also saw how to declare nested functions, and what is meant by closures. Finally, you learned how to declare recursive functions.

Chapter 8 will show you how to carry out object orientation in JS.

CHAPTER 8

■ ■ ■

Object-Oriented Programming in JavaScript

As with ABAP, JavaScript allows you to create objects. However, the concepts pertaining to object creation in the two languages are not the same. This chapter covers object creation, instantiation, and inheritance in JS. After starting with an overview of object-oriented programming (OOP) in general, the rest of the chapter shows how OOP is implemented in JS, along with relevant syntax. It introduces the this operator in detail, then covers the various ways of creating objects, followed by the instantiation steps using the new keyword. Once you have a basic understanding of objects, the chapter moves on to inheritance as implemented in JS using prototypes. This chapter presents real-life examples of objects and subobjects throughout, along with sample code listings used for implementing them in JavaScript.

For brevity's sake, only the JS code is shown in this chapter. By now, you are fully aware that this code needs HTML tags in order to execute in a browser.

Object-Oriented Programming in General

To understand object-oriented programming in JavaScript, you need to understand object-oriented programming in general.

In OOP, you use the concept of objects to model real-life objects inside programs. The conceptual object may contain data and code that relate to the real-life object that you have modeled, or the features (behavior) that developers want the object to exhibit. For example, you can have a Player class that contains a number of properties (attributes) and a function sayhello() method, as shown in Figure 8-1.

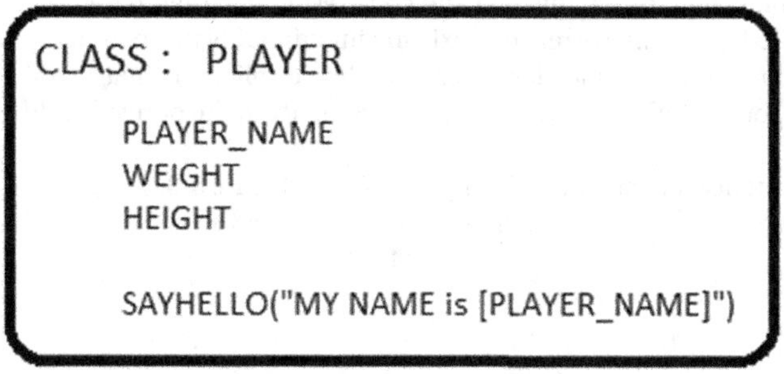

```
CLASS :  PLAYER

       PLAYER_NAME
       WEIGHT
       HEIGHT

       SAYHELLO("MY NAME is [PLAYER_NAME]")
```

Figure 8-1. *Class Player*

© Rehan Zaidi 2017
R. Zaidi, *JavaScript Essentials for SAP ABAP Developers*, DOI 10.1007/978-1-4842-2220-1_8

This object representation is called a *class*. (In JS, however, a different mechanism is used, as described a bit later.) A class may be considered a template that specifies the properties that an object originating from it must have.

You can create a number of instances of a class. These objects comprise the data and features specified in the class definition. For example, for the Player class, you can create any number of players, as shown in Figure 8-2. While creating an object, the constructor function of the class is executed in order to create the new object instance. This is called *instantiation*.

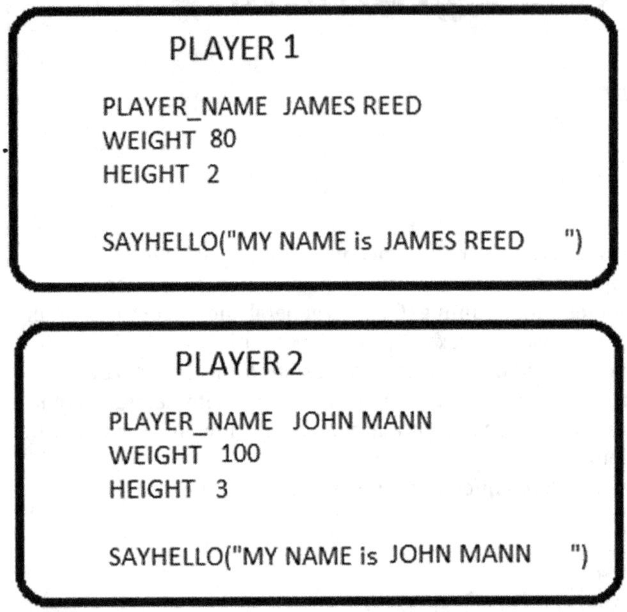

```
PLAYER 1

PLAYER_NAME  JAMES REED
WEIGHT  80
HEIGHT  2


SAYHELLO("MY NAME is  JAMES REED      ")
```

```
PLAYER 2

PLAYER_NAME   JOHN MANN
WEIGHT   100
HEIGHT   3


SAYHELLO("MY NAME is  JOHN MANN      ")
```

Figure 8-2. *Instances of Player*

The Player class shown in Figure 8-2 has two instances, player1 and player2, each having its own player_name, weight, and height properties, as well as a different text string in the sayhello() method.

Taking this example one step further, suppose you don't want to allow creation of general players, meaning no one can be just a "player." Each person must choose to be a specific type of player, such as a cricket player or a football player. Within the OOP arena, it is possible to create new classes from existing classes. The new classes, called child classes, may then inherit the data and code residing in their parent class (i.e., the class from which they are inherited). This allows reuse of existing functionality in a parent class (which comprises data and code common among its child classes), rather than duplicating that functionality in a number of separate classes. You may also add additional functionality to the derived child classes, if needed.

To better understand the concept of inheritance, consider the example shown in Figure 8-3.

```
CRICKET PLAYER

    PLAYER_NAME
    WEIGHT
    HEIGHT
    COUNTY_NAME
    SAYHELLO(" I PLAY CRICKET            ")
```

```
FOOTBALL  PLAYER

    PLAYER_NAME
    WEIGHT
    HEIGHT
    CLUB_NAME
    SAYHELLO(" I PLAY FOOTBALL          ")
```

Figure 8-3. *Cricket Player and Football Player child classes*

The Cricket Player and Football Player classes have many properties in common, such as player_ name, weight, and age, so it is easier to define all those properties in the parent class Player and create Cricket Player and Football Player as child classes that inherit those properties.

It is also possible to specify a given feature differently in these classes. For example, the sayhello() text of the Cricket Player child class might be "I am a cricket Player", whereas the sayhello() text of the Football Player child class might be "I am a football Player". The capability to implement the same feature differently in different object types is known as *polymorphism*.

It is now possible to create instances from these child classes, such as CricketPlayer1, CricketPlayer2, FootballPlayer1, and so on.

Object Instances and Constructors

JavaScript is not a typical object-oriented programming language. Other OOP languages have a class statement (definition) for defining classes. Using these classes, objects may be created that contain the properties and methods contained in the class. By contrast, JS uses special functions known as *constructors* to define object properties and methods. One constructor may be used to create any number of objects, with an option to add additional functions and data to them.

If you create a new instance using a constructor, the features available within the constructor are linked through a prototype chain. (This is unlike other OOP languages, where all functionalities are copied from the class to the new instantiated object.)

This section shows you four different approaches to simulate object creation in JS (using the Player object as a real-life example):

- Using an object literal

- Using a constructor function

- Using the Object() constructor

- Using the create() method

Approach 1: Using an Object Literal

The first approach is to use a function that uses an object literal. A function that deals with the player example is shown in Listing 8-1.

Listing 8-1. Using an Object Literal

```
function defineaPlayer(pname,weight, height) {
  var myobj = {};
  myobj.name = pname;
  myobj.weight = weight;
  myobj.height = height;
  myobj.sayhello = function() {
    alert('Hi, my name is ' + this.pname + '.');
  };
  return myobj;
}
```

Here, the function `myPlayer` takes as input `pname`, `weight`, and `height`. An object `myobj` is defined within the `myPlayer` function, and then properties such as name, weight, and height are added. Listing 8-1 also defines a `sayhello` method. Finally, the function returns the `myobj` object.

You can then create a new player using a call to this function:

```
var player =  defineaPlayer('James Watson', 100,50);
console.log(player.pname);
console.log(player.sayhello());
```

Although this arrangement works, it is lengthy and unnecessarily declares an empty object and returns it.

Approach 2: Using a Constructor Function

JavaScript provides another short way to object creation using constructor functions. You can define a constructor function for the player example as shown in Listing 8-2.

Listing 8-2. Player Constructor Function

```
function Player(pname,weight, height) {
  this.name = pname;
  this.weight = weight;
  this.height = height;
  this.sayhello = function() {
    alert('Hi, my name is ' + this.pname + '.');
  };
```

■ **Note**   A constructor function in JavaScript is similar to a class (reserved word `class`) in other OOP languages.

A constructor function defines the methods and properties pertaining to the object. The this keyword is used to assign values to the property of the object being created. A major difference between approach 1 (using an object literal) and approach 2 is that the latter uses the this keyword. This means that whenever an object is created using a constructor function, the various properties identified will be equal to the corresponding parameters passed via the constructor call.

Consider the following example:

```
var player1 = new Player('James', 100, 20);
var player2 = new Player('John', 120, 60);
```

The following statements will then work:

```
player1.pname
player2.pname
```

This example creates two objects, player 1 and player2. They have property pname and method sayhello, but these are stored separately and do not collide with one another. In each case, the new keyword is used to create a new object instance, followed by various parameters in brackets. Each object instance is created using Player, as shown in Listing 8-3.

Listing 8-3. Player Example

```
function Player(pname,weight, height) {
  this.name = pname;
  this.weight = weight;
  this.height = height;
  this.sayhello = function() {
    alert('Hi, my name is ' + this.pname + '.');
  };
}
```

Once the new objects are created, player1 and player2 (in actual effect) contain the following:

```
{
  name : James;
  weight : 100;
  height : 20;
  sayhello : function() {
    alert('Hi, my name is ' + this.pname + '.');
  };
}

{
  name : John;
  weight : 120;
  height : 60;
  sayhello : function() {
    alert('Hi, my name is ' + this.pname + '.');
  };
}
```

Approach 3: Using the Object() Constructor

A third way to create objects is to use the Object() constructor. Consider the following code:

```
var player1 = new Object();
```

This has an empty object created under the player1 variable. Once this is done, you can then add methods and properties to the object. For this, you can use either brackets or a dot, as shown here:

```
player1.pname = 'John';
player1.weight = 100;
player1['height'] = 30;
player1.sayhello = function() {
 alert('My name is ' + this.pname) ;
};
```

It is also possible to pass a literal while calling the Object() constructor and specify the properties and methods. This is more compact and understandable, as shown in Listing 8-4.

Listing 8-4. Using the Object() Constructor

```
var player1 = new Object({
  pname: 'John',
  height: 100,
  weight: 20,
  sayhello: function() {
    alert('My name is' + this.pname + '.');
  }
});

player1.sayhello();
```

As you can see, one statement in Listing 8-4 calls the Object() constructor and specifies the values of the properties and method, all together. The statement has the same effect as the previous code block. The output of the code is shown in Figure 8-4.

Figure 8-4. *Output of program using the Object() constructor*

Approach 4: Using the create() Method

The JS language has a method known as create() that lets you create an object instance from an existing object. A code example is shown here:

```
var player2 = Object.create(player1);
```

Here, the existing object is player1. The create method of Object is used to create an exactly identical object, player2 (i.e., it has the same properties and methods available in player1). Once the preceding statement has been executed, the following statements will work and provide the same output if used for player1:

```
console.log(player2.pname);
player2.sayhello();
```

This approach is very useful and enables developers to create new instances based on another instance.

JavaScript: A Prototype-Based Language

As mentioned earlier in this chapter, in traditional OOP, classes are defined. When objects are instantiated from a class, the properties and methods residing in the class are copied to the newly created instance. However, in JavaScript this is not the case. JS uses the mechanism of *prototypes* to implement object orientation.

JavaScript objects inherit features differently as compared to other OOP languages. This section demonstrates this difference, describes how prototype chains function, and shows how the prototype property may be used to add methods to existing constructor functions.

JavaScript is a prototype-based language. That means each object, let's say A, has an object named prototype that is an object from which the object derives properties and methods. Likewise, object A's prototype object may also have a prototype object, and so on. This is known as a *chain of prototypes*. In JavaScript, the methods and properties reside on the object's constructor. A connection is created between the instance and the constructor of the object.

To better understand the prototype concept, consider the following example, which has a simple Player function:

```
function Player(pname,weight,height)
{
}
```

Next, an object instance, player1, is created:

```
var player1 = new Player('James', 100 , 20);
```

Displaying the contents of player1 in the web browser console results in the output shown in Figure 8-5.

Figure 8-5. *Console output of player1*

As you can see, the members residing in the player1 prototype objects are pname, weight, and height. These reside on the Player constructor's prototype object, which is Object. See Figure 8-6.

Figure 8-6. *Player1, Player, and Object*

Suppose you call a method using player1 that resides in Object, such as valueOf. In this case , JS first checks whether the Player1 object has the method valueOf. Because this is not true, JS next searches the Player object for the valueOf method. The method does not exist in the Player object either. Therefore, JS then searches the prototype object of Player's constructor. (This is Object.) Object contains the given method you are searching for.

To better understand the inheritance of properties, take a look at Object in console.log.

A large number of properties exist in Object. However, all of them are not available in the player1 object. The properties that are inherited reside on the prototype property of Object. (i.e., they do not simply start with Object but with Object.prototype). The "value" of the property of "prototype" is actually an object that contains a set of properties and methods that may be inherited down the inheritance (prototype) chain. For example, the method Object.prototype.valueOf() is present in any objects that are inherited from Object. On the other hand, the method Object.key is not inherited by objects that are inherited from Object.

Returning to the example shown earlier, the prototype of Player is shown in Figure 8-7.

```
▼ Object ⊡
  ▶ constructor: Player(name,weight,height)
  ▼ __proto__: Object
    ▶ __defineGetter__: __defineGetter__()
    ▶ __defineSetter__: __defineSetter__()
    ▶ __lookupGetter__: __lookupGetter__()
    ▶ __lookupSetter__: __lookupSetter__()
    ▶ constructor: Object()
    ▶ hasOwnProperty: hasOwnProperty()
    ▶ isPrototypeOf: isPrototypeOf()
    ▶ propertyIsEnumerable: propertyIsEnumerable()
    ▶ toLocaleString: toLocaleString()
    ▶ toString: toString()
    ▶ valueOf: valueOf()
    ▶ get __proto__: __proto__()
    ▶ set __proto__: __proto__()
```

Figure 8-7. *Prototype of Player*

Not too many things exist in Figure 8-7 because no methods have been defined on the Player constructor.

Next, take a look at Object.prototype displayed using the Chrome console, shown in Figure 8-8.

```
▼ Object ⊡
  ▶ __defineGetter__: __defineGetter__()
  ▶ __defineSetter__: __defineSetter__()
  ▶ __lookupGetter__: __lookupGetter__()
  ▶ __lookupSetter__: __lookupSetter__()
  ▶ constructor: Object()
  ▶ hasOwnProperty: hasOwnProperty()
  ▶ isPrototypeOf: isPrototypeOf()
  ▶ propertyIsEnumerable: propertyIsEnumerable()
  ▶ toLocaleString: toLocaleString()
  ▶ toString: toString()
  ▶ valueOf: valueOf()
  ▶ get __proto__: __proto__()
  ▶ set __proto__: __proto__()
```

Figure 8-8. *Object.prototype*

Suppose you add the following statement:

```
var another_player  = Object.create(player1);
```

The create method of Object creates a new object from a prototype object.

As you can see, player2 has been created using player1. Suppose you enter the following:

```
console.log(another_player.__proto__);
```

The output of the statement is shown in Figure 8-9.

```
▼ Player 🔳
    height: 20
    pname: "John"
    weight: 100
  ▼ __proto__: Object
    ▶ constructor: Player(name,weight,height)
    ▶ __proto__: Object
```

Figure 8-9. *__proto__ of*

Each object has a property named `constructor` that links to the constructor function (used for creating the instance). The output of `player1.constructor` and `player2.constructor` is shown in Figure 8-10.

```
function Player(name,weight,height)
{

  this.pname = name;
  this.weight = weight;
  this.height = height;

} function Player(name,weight,height)
{

  this.pname = name;
  this.weight = weight;
  this.height = height;

}
```

Figure 8-10. *Player1 and Player2 Constructor*

As you can see, both of these return the `Player` constructor.

It is also possible to create a new instance using the `constructor` property (along with necessary parameters). Consider this example:

```
var player3 =  new player1.constructor('John Mann', 100, 11);
```

This example uses the `constructor` property as a function including parentheses in conjunction with the new keyword.

When you output the contents of the new object, `player3`, as shown next, it works correctly:

```
player3.pname
player3.weight
person3.height
```

The constructor property can be used in yet another way. You can modify the prototype property of constructor to add a new method to the prototype of the constructor:

```
Player.prototype.hello = function(){
    alert('I am Player');
}
Player1.hello();
```

Running the hello method will display an alert message saying I am Player. It is worth noting that the entire chain of inheritance may be changed at runtime, thus making the hello() method available on all instances derived from constructor Player.

To better understand, consider the following code:

```
function Player(pname, weight, height) {
 this.pname = pname;  this.height = height; this.weight = weight;
};
var player1 = new Player('James', 32,100);
Player.prototype.hello = function() {
   alert('I am' + this.pname);
}
player1.hello();
```

This example begins with a constructor Player and then defines a new method hello using the prototype property of Player. The method is available on the player1 object instance. The functionality has been updated automatically. As mentioned earlier, this confirms the prototype chain. JS first looks for the method in the object instance, then moves upward on the prototype chain.

Another way to define properties is to use the prototype property. For example, you can add a city property to the Player object:

```
Player.prototype.city = 'New York';
```

However, this is not very common. A more common approach is to specify properties inside the constructor whereas the various methods using the prototype. In this case, the code is easy to understand, as all properties reside within the constructor and the methods are defined in different blocks later:

```
function Player(a, b, c, d) {
  // property definitions
};

Player.prototype.func1 = function() { ... }
Player.prototype.func2 = function() { ... }
```

Prototypal Inheritance

Now that you have some idea of inheritance and the working prototype, you are ready to see these concepts in action. As already mentioned earlier, JavaScript uses prototype-based inheritance. This involves linking the inherited object using a prototype chain. This section shows you a technique for implementing the concept of inheritance in JavaScript.

Starting with the Player constructor created earlier, keep in mind that only the properties pname, weight, and height are specified within Player:

```
function Player(pname, weight, height) {
  this.pname = pname;
  this.weight = weight;
  this.height = height;
};
```

Now, define a method tellname on the constructor's prototype property:

```
Player.prototype.tellname = function() {
  alert('My name is ' + this.pname + ' and I am a Player' );
};
```

The function tellname will show the name of the player in an alert box.

Next, suppose you want to create a constructor named CricketPlayer that inherits all the members of Player defined earlier. In addition, you want it to contain a new property named cricketcounty and an updated method named tellme.

First, create a CricketPlayer constructor as shown:

```
function CricketPlayer(pname, weight, height, cricketcounty) {
  Player.call(this, pname, weight, height);
  this.cricketcounty = cricketcounty;
}
```

■ **Note**   Having a lot of levels of inheritance is not recommended. Too many levels may cause a lot of confusion as well as lot of hard work when debugging. As you will see, the call() method enables you to call a function residing outside the constructor but within the same context.

The call method is used for chaining constructors. In this case, it calls the constructor of Player. The first parameter, this, points to the current function, and the rest of the parameters are used to supply values for the called function (i.e., Player constructor) parameters.

At the end is the cricketcounty property that is not in Player but only specific to the CricketPlayer function. In effect, you are executing the Player constructor function within the CricketPlayer constructor function.

This is the same as the following block of code:

```
function CricketPlayer(pname, weight, height, cricketcounty) {
  this.pname = pname ;
  this.weight = weight ;
  this.height = height;
  this.cricketcounty = cricketcounty;
}
```

However, this does not include the reusability feature, so you shouldn't use it.

Now that you have a constructor that has a prototype property that points to the constructor function, add the following line so that the CricketPlayer() function inherits the methods defined in the Player's prototype property:

```
CricketPlayer.prototype = Object.create(Player.prototype);
```

Here, the create method is used to create a new object based on the value pointed to by Player. prototype. The new object is assigned to CricketPlayer.prototype so that CricketPlayer.prototype inherits the method in Player.prototype. Until this point, CricketPlayer.prototype is equal to Player() (because CricketPlayer.prototype is assigned to an object that is a Player.prototype object). This may be problematic, so you need to add the following statement at the end:

```
CricketPlayer.prototype.constructor = CricketPlayer;
CricketPlayer.prototype.tellname = function() {
    alert('My name is ' + this.pname + 'and I am a cricket Player of' + this.cricketcounty +
'.' );
};
```

At the end, you may add the following statements:

```
var cper = new CricketPlayer('Jon Reed', 100, 190, ' Surrey County');
cper.tellname();
```

The complete inheritance code is shown in Listing 8-5.

Listing 8-5. Complete Inheritance Code

```
<html>
   <body>
      <script>

function Player(pname, weight, height) {
  this.pname = pname;
  this.weight = weight;
  this.height = height;
};

function CricketPlayer(pname, weight, height, cricketcounty) {
  Player.call(this, pname, weight, height);
  this.cricketcounty = cricketcounty;
}

Player.prototype.tellname = function() {
   alert('My name is ' + this.pname + ' and I am a Player' );
};

CricketPlayer.prototype = Object.create(Player.prototype);
CricketPlayer.prototype.constructor = CricketPlayer;

CricketPlayer.prototype.tellname = function() {
   alert('My name is ' + this.pname + ' and I am a cricket Player of' + this.cricketcounty +
'.' );
};
```

```
var per = new Player('James Wood', 120,20);
var cper = new CricketPlayer('Jon Reed', 100, 190, ' Surrey County');
per.tellname();
cper.tellname();

    </script>
  </body>
</html>
```

At this point, the per and cper contents are as shown in Figure 8-11.

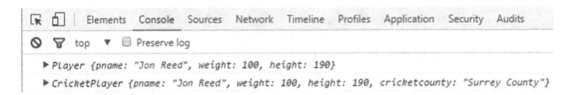

Figure 8-11. *Content of per and cper in console.log*

The first three members, pname, height, and weight, were inherited from Player, whereas cricketcounty was defined at the CricketPlayer level. The method tellname was redefined at the CricketPlayer level.

At the end of Listing 8-5, two objects, per and cper, are defined using the new keyword, and then the tellname method is called for the objects per and cper. This invokes different methods each time. As a result, two different alert boxes are presented, as shown in Figures 8-12 and 8-13.

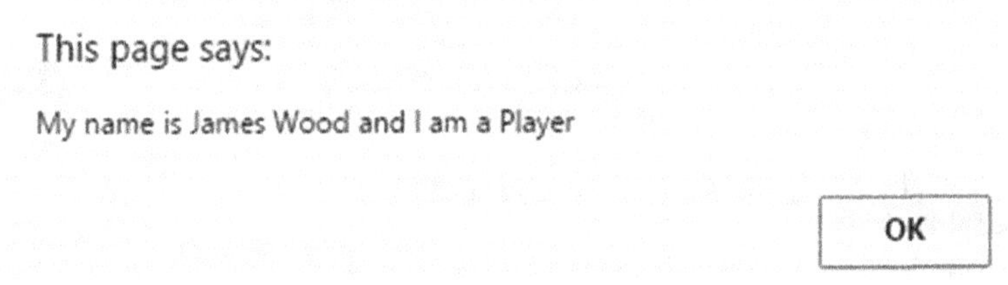

This page says:

My name is James Wood and I am a Player

OK

Figure 8-12. *Method tellname output of class Player*

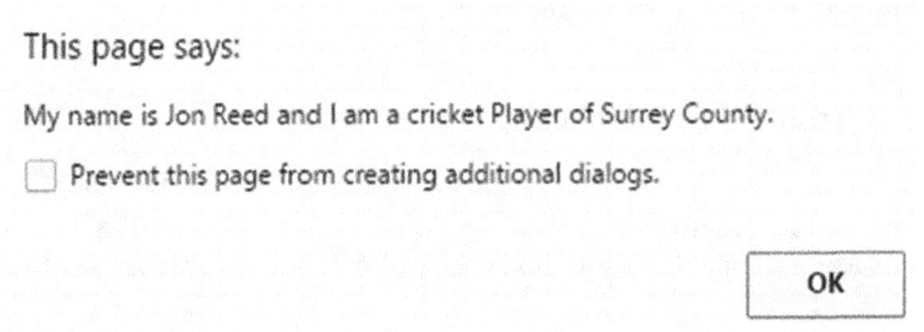

This page says:

My name is Jon Reed and I am a cricket Player of Surrey County.

☐ Prevent this page from creating additional dialogs.

OK

Figure 8-13. *Method tellname output of class Cricket Player*

As you can see, the outputs of the two methods are entirely in different formats. This is a demonstration of polymorphism.

Summary

This chapter first provided a general overview of object-oriented programming, and then showed you how OOP is implemented in JS, along with relevant syntax. It covered the `this` operator, then covered the various ways of creating objects, followed by the instantiation steps using the `new` keyword. The chapter wrapped up with an introduction to inheritance as implemented in JS using prototypes.

In Chapter 9, you will see a number of built-in objects of JS in detail, and the properties and methods they provide that can be used by JS developers to reduce their programming time and efforts.

CHAPTER 9

Objects

In JavaScript, an object is an unordered list of properties. A property is composed of a name and a value and can also be a function. In this case, the function is called a method. This chapter covers some of the standard objects you need to be familiar with when coding with JavaScript. It also presents examples of their properties and the methods you are most likely to use with them. The chapter also covers arrays, Boolean objects, string objects, and date objects.

Objects Revisited

Listing 9-1 presents a simple example of an object.

Listing 9-1. Object Example

```html
<html>
   <body>
      <script>
         var book = {novel: "Secret", author: "Rhonda Byrne", publicationDate: "Nov 2006"};
         console.log(book.novel + " this book is of author " + book.author);
      </script>
   </body>
</html>
```

As this example shows, an object contains a list of items, and each item in the list has a name-value pair. The properties' names are `novel`, `author`, and `publicationDate`, each of which is assigned a value. The output of this code is shown in Figure 9-1.

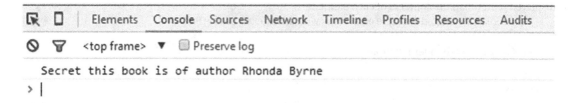

Figure 9-1. Output

Array

As you saw earlier in the book, an array object lets you store multiple values under a single variable name. The index number starts with 0, and the first element of an array is represented as [0], the second as [1], and so on.

The syntax of an array creation is

```
var arrayName = [value1, value2, .... Valuen]
```

Consider the simple example of an array literal in Listing 9-2.

Listing 9-2. Array Literal Example

```
<html>
   <body>
      <script>
          var countries = ["India", "Germany", "Scotland"];
          console.log(countries);
      </script>
   </body>
</html>
```

This example declares the variable `countries` as an array, and it contains the elements India, Germany, and Scotland. Next, the `console.log` method is used to print the `countries` array. As you can see, this example does not specify any index or element to be printed. This code gives you the maximum length of an array.

The output of Listing 9-2 is shown in Figure 9-2.

Figure 9-2. *Output*

If no element index of an array is specified in a `console.log` statement, the total number of elements is displayed rather than the contents of each element.

Now consider a related example of an array with an index in Listing 9-3.

Listing 9-3. Array with Index Example

```
<html>
   <body>
      <script>
          var countries = ["India", "Germany", "Scotland"];
          console.log(countries[0], countries[1], countries[2]);
      </script>
   </body>
</html>
```

Using the same starting base code as in Listing 9-2, this example shows how you can gain access to the various elements of the array by specifying the array index number. The output of this code is shown in Figure 9-3.

Figure 9-3. *Output*

Arrays may also be defined using a new keyword, as shown in the example in Listing 9-4.

Listing 9-4. New Array with Index Example

```html
<html>
  <body>
    <script>
        var countries = new Array( "India", "Germany", "Scotland" );
        console.log(countries[0], countries[1], countries[2]);
    </script>
  </body>
</html>
```

This takes the same initial example and adds the keyword new. Both examples work exactly the same way; the only the difference is that Listing 9-4 creates a new array. The output of this code is shown in Figure 9-4.

Figure 9-4. *Output*

■ **Note**   When possible, create arrays without a new keyword—it's faster.

Properties of Array Object

The three most commonly used properties of the array object are listed and described in Table 9-1.

Table 9-1. *Properties of the Array Object*

Property	Description
constructor	Returns array function
index	Returns the zero-based index of the match in the string
length	Gives the length of an array

The `constructor` and `length` properties are described in more detail next.

Property constructor

The syntax of the `constructor` property is

`array.constructor`

This returns the function `Array() { [native code] }`. A simple example of this is shown in Listing 9-5.

Listing 9-5. Array constructor Property Example

```
<html>
    <body>
        <script>
                var countries = new Array( "Germany", "India", "Scotland" );
                console.log("countries.constructor is:" + countries.constructor);
        </script>
    </body>
</html>
```

This example declares the array `countries` with the new keyword and then uses `console.log` to display `countries.constructor`. The output of this code is shown in Figure 9-5.

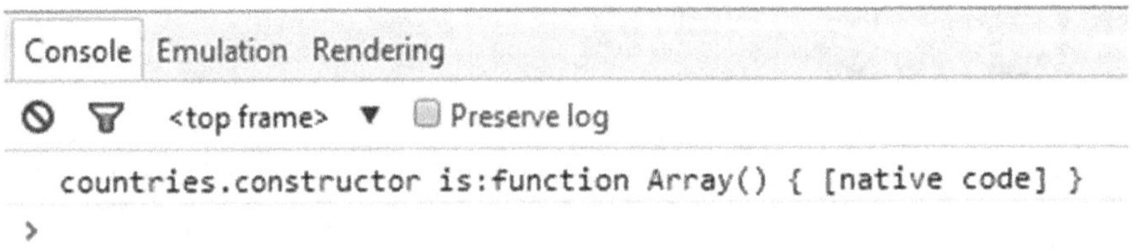

| Console | Emulation | Rendering |

🚫 ▽ <top frame> ▼ ☐ Preserve log

countries.constructor is:function Array() { [native code] }

\>

Figure 9-5. *Output*

Property length

As the name indicates, the `length` property contains the length of the array. The number of elements is specified in integer form. The syntax of a length property is

`array.length`

This returns the array length—the total number of elements. Listing 9-6 provides a working example of this property in action.

Listing 9-6. Array length Property Example

```html
<html>
    <body>
        <script>
                var countries = new Array( "Germany", "India", "Scotland", "Austria" );
                console.log("Length of array is:" + countries.length);
        </script>
    </body>
</html>
```

The output of Listing 9-6 is shown in Figure 9-6.

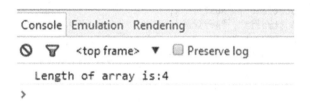

Figure 9-6. *Output*

Array Methods

The array object contains a number of methods, several of which are listed and described in Table 9-2.

Table 9-2. *Methods of the Array Object*

Method	Description
concat()	Combines two or more arrays and returns the new one.
forEach()	Executes the specified function for each element in an array.
join()	Combines the elements of an array into a string.
lastIndexOf()	Returns the last index at which the given element is found within the array. If the element is not in the array, -1 is returned.
pop()	Removes and returns the last element of the array.
push()	Adds one or more elements to the end of the array and returns the new array length.
reverse()	Reverses the order of the array.
toString()	Returns the components of the array in string form.
sort()	Sorts the array elements.
shift()	Removes the first element and returns the updated array.
slice()	Cuts out a portion of the array as specified by the positions, and returns the array in a form of a string.

More detailed descriptions of the concat and pop methods follow.

Method concat

The syntax of the concat() method is

```
array.concat(arr1, arr2, ..., arrN);
```

Here, arr1 and arr2 are the elements of array. This returns another array with concatenated values. Listing 9-7 show an example of this method is used.

Listing 9-7. Array concat() Method Example

```html
<html>
   <body>
     <script>
             var countries = ["Germany", "Scotland", "Austria"];
             var continents = ["Europe", "Australia", "Africa"];
             var world = countries.concat(continents);
             console.log(" The world map has countries & continents:" + world);
     </script>
   </body>
</html>
```

This example declares two arrays, one with variable countries and the other with variable continents. The concat() method is then used to combine these two array elements and form a new array.

The output of Listing 9-7 is shown in Figure 9-7.

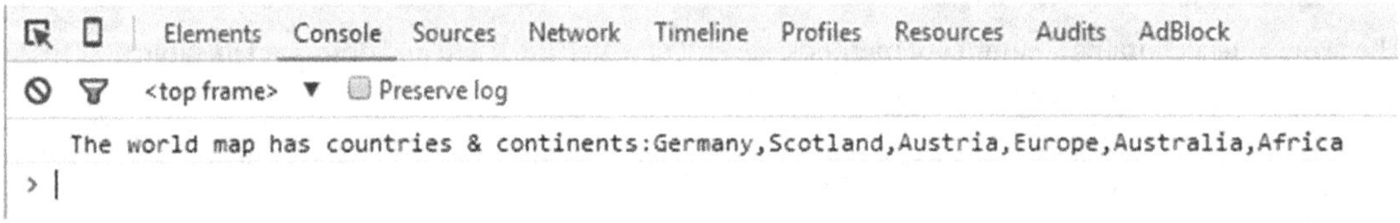

Figure 9-7. *Output*

Method pop

The pop method removes the last element from an array and returns its value. The syntax of the pop() method is

```
array.pop();
```

This returns the element or value that is removed from the array. Listing 9-8 provides an example of the pop() method.

Listing 9-8. Array pop() Method Example

```
<html>
   <body>
      <script>
               var countries = ["Germany", "Scotland", "Austria"];
               var value = countries.pop();
               console.log(" Removed value from array is:" + value);
               var value = countries.pop();
               console.log(" Removed value from array is:" + value);
      </script>
   </body>
</html>
```

This example declares the variable countries with some array elements and then uses the pop() method. This value is stored in the variable value and then displayed. The output of this code is shown in Figure 9-8.

Figure 9-8. *Output*

Boolean

A Boolean object represents two values: true or false. The syntax of a Boolean is

```
Boolean (value)
```

Listing 9-9 shows an example of the Boolean object.

Listing 9-9. Boolean Object Example

```
<html>
   <body>
      <script>

            function myBoolean() {
            console.log(10 < 15);
            }
            myBoolean();
      </script>
   </body>
</html>
```

This example compares the Boolean values. If 10 is less than 15, the code returns true; if not, it returns false. The output of Listing 9-9 is shown in Figure 9-9.

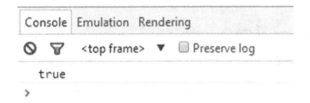

Figure 9-9. *Output*

Boolean Properties

The properties of a Boolean object are listed and described in Table 9-3.

Table 9-3. *Boolean Properties*

Property	Description
constructor	Constructor of the object
prototype	Lets developers add properties and methods

Boolean Methods

Let us now discuss some of the useful methods of Boolean objects.

Method valueOf

The syntax of the valueOf() method is

```
boolean.valueOf()
```

This returns the primitive value of the specified Boolean object. Listing 9-10 shows an example of this.

Listing 9-10. Boolean valueOf() Method Example

```
<html>
   <body>
     <script>
             var value = Boolean(10 < 15);
             var num = value.valueOf();
             console.log( "Value of Boolean is:" + num.valueOf() );
     </script>
   </body>
</html>
```

This example assigns the variable value and then uses the method valueOf() to check whether the Boolean expression is true or false. The output is shown in Figure 9-10.

Figure 9-10. *Output*

String

In a string object, you can store a series of characters, like this example:

```
var textString = "JavaScript language" or 'JavaScript language'
```

As shown, you can write this series either in single quotation marks or double quotation marks.

String Properties

Some of the properties of a string object are listed and described in Table 9-4.

Table 9-4. *Properties of a String Object*

Property	Description
length	The length of the string
constructor	Returns a reference to the string function
prototype	Lets developers add properties and methods to the object

A more detailed description of the length property follows.

Property length

The syntax of property length is

```
string.length
```

This gives you the number of characters in the string, including spaces and blanks. Consider the simple example in Listing 9-11.

Listing 9-11. String length Property Example

```html
<html>
    <body>
        <script>
                var text = "JavaScript Object";
                var strLength = text.length;
                console.log( "The string length is:" + strLength );
        </script>
    </body>
</html>
```

This example shows the length of the string. It declares the variable text and assigns a string to it. Then, using the property length, it identifies the number of characters in the given string. The output of this code is shown in Figure 9-11.

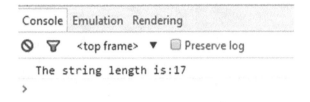

Figure 9-11. *Output*

String Methods

String methods are listed and described in Table 9-5.

Table 9-5. *String Methods*

Method	Description
concat()	Combines two or more strings.
indexOf()	Searches the string for the given text and starting position within the main string. It returns -1 if the search is not successful.
match()	Returns "match string" when matching a string against a regular expression.
replace()	Replaces a string with a new string after checking regular expressions.
charAt()	Returns the character at a given position.
slice()	Removes characters and extracts a portion of the string based on the specified start and end positions (the end character is not included).
split()	Separates the string into a number of substrings based on a given separator such as ',' and returns them in an array.
search()	Searches through the string for a value or regular expression. If found, the matched position is then returned.
toUpperCase()	Converts to uppercase.
toLowerCase()	Converts to lowercase.
substr()	Also used for extraction. However, the starting position and the number of characters to be extracted are specified.
Includes()	Checks if a string contains a certain character or set of characters.
endsWith()	Checks if the string ends with a certain character or set of characters.

The chartAt, repeat, and slice methods are described in more detail next.

Method charAt

The syntax for method charAt() is

```
String.charAt(ind)
```

This returns the character at the given position. Consider the chartAt() example in Listing 9-12.

Listing 9-12. String charAt() Method Example

```
<html>
    <body>
      <script>
              var text = "JavaScript Object";
              var char = text.charAt(2);
              console.log( "The character at position 2 is:" + char );
      </script>
    </body>
</html>
```

We've now used the same example to show the method charAt(), which identifies the character at the given index number. (Note that arrays have base 0, so if you put 2 as an index, you will get the third character.)

The output of Listing 9-12 is shown in Figure 9-12.

Figure 9-12. *Output*

Method repeat

The syntax of method repeat is

```
String.repeat(n)
```

Here, the number of times the string content is to be repeated is specified via the number n. This returns the string containing the repeated text. To better understand how this works, consider the example in Listing 9-13.

Listing 9-13. String repeat() Method Example

```html
<html>
  <body>
    <script>
            var text = "JavaScript Object";
            var string = text.repeat(2);
            console.log( "The string repeats twice:" + string );
    </script>
  </body>
</html>
```

In this case, the declared string "JavaScript Object" is written twice through the method repeat(). The output of this code is shown in Figure 9-13.

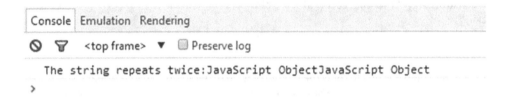

Figure 9-13. *Output*

Method slice

The syntax of method slice is

```
string.slice( startslice [, endSlice] );
```

Here, startslice is the starting position number of the portion to be extracted before it is removed, and endslice is optional and is used to remove part of the string from the right side. The index (position) is specified from the right side of the string (i.e., counts from the end of the string and to the left). Everything after this is removed and not sent as part of the returned string. This number is passed as a negative sign. So, -4 denotes last four characters.

Consider the example of the slice method in Listing 9-14.

Listing 9-14. String slice() Method Example

```html
<html>
  <body>
    <script>
            var text = "JavaScript is also Object oriented";
            var string = text.slice(4, -4);
            console.log( "The new string is:" + string );
    </script>
  </body>
</html>
```

This example declares the variable text and assigns it with the string. The starting and ending index numbers are specified in the slice method, and the code will extract the characters between them from the string. The output is shown in Figure 9-14.

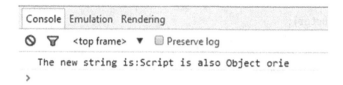

Figure 9-14. *Output*

Date

Date objects help us work with dates and times. There are four ways to create this object:

```
new Date( )
new Date(milliseconds)
new Date(datestring)
new Date(year,month,date[,hour,minute,second,millisecond ])
```

Date Properties

Date properties are listed and described in Table 9-6.

Table 9-6. *Date Properties*

Property	Description
constructor	Constructor
prototype	Lets developers add properties and methods

Property constructor

The constructor property returns the function that creates the date object prototype. The syntax of the constructor is

```
date.constructor
```

Consider the example of the constructor property in Listing 9-15.

Listing 9-15. Date constructor Property Example

```html
<html>
  <body>
    <script>
            var tdyDate = new Date();
            console.log(tdyDate.constructor);
    </script>
  </body>
</html>
```

This example declares the variable tdyDate with a new date. The constructor property returns the function date. The output is shown in Figure 9-15.

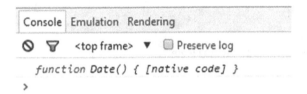

Figure 9-15. *Code output*

Date Methods

Some of the commonly used methods for date objects are listed and described in Table 9-7.

Table 9-7. *Methods for Date Objects*

Method	Description
getDate()	Gives the day of the month in the date (e.g., 1 , 2 , 3, ... 31)
getDay()	Gives the weekday in the form of number (e.g., from 0, 1, 2, ... 6)
getFullYear()	Returns the year in the date (e.g., 1978)
getHours()	Gives the hour of the date (e.g., 0 , 1, ... 23)
getMinutes()	Returns the minutes of the date (e.g., 0, 1, 2, ... 59)
getMonth()	Gives the month of the date object (e.g., 0, 1, 2, 11)
getSeconds()	Returns the seconds (e.g., 0, 1, 2, 3, ... 59)

For all the methods in Table 9-7 except getDay(), there is a corresponding set method, such as setDate, setFullYear, and so on.

Let's now look at a few examples.

Using Property prototype with Method getDay()

As already mentioned, the prototype property allows you to add properties and methods to an object, whether it is a Boolean, string, date, or another. The syntax to use the prototype property is

```
Object.prototype.name = value
```

Listing 9-16 shows how you can add a new method to a date object.

Listing 9-16. Date prototype Property Example

```html
<html>
    <body>
        <script>
            function myDay() {
                var tdyDay = new Date();
                tdyDay.today();
                console.log(tdyDay.Day);
            }
              Date.prototype.today = function() {
              switch (this.getDay()) {
              case 0:
                      this.Day = "Sunday";
                      break;
              case 1:
                      this.Day = "Monday";
                      break;
              case 2:
                      this.Day = "Tuesday";
                      break;
              case 3:
                      this.Day = "Wednesday";
                      break;
               case 4:
                      this.Day = "Thursday";
                      break;
               case 5:
                      this.Day = "Friday";
                      break;
              case 6:
                      this.Day = "Saturday";
                      break;
              }
          };
          myDay();
        </script>
    </body>
</html>
```

This example adds a new function today to the date object. Within this function, first the getDay function finds out the number representing the day using. Based on this, the name of the day—such as 0 for Monday, 1 for Tuesday, and so on—is displayed. Within the function myDay, a new date is defined and the today method is called.

The output of Listing 9-16 is shown in Figure 9-16.

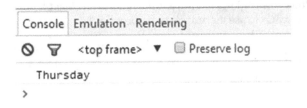

Figure 9-16. Output

Method setMonth

The syntax of the setMonth() method is

```
Date.setMonth(monthValue[, dayValue])
```

Here, monthValue represents months from January to December, but the integer value passed for it must be from 0 to 11, where 0 represents January and so on. The dayValue parameter is optional and represents the date of the month, for example 1, 2, 3 … 31.

Listing 9-17 shows how you can use this method in a program.

Listing 9-17. Date setMonth() Method Example

```html
<html>
   <body>
      <script>
            var d1 = new Date( "March 23, 2017 11:35:00" );
            d1.setMonth( 1 );
            console.log( "The date is set to: " + d1 );
      </script>
   </body>
</html>
```

This example declares a date d1 and assigns a value to it using the new keyword. It then calls the method setMonth() and passes the value 1. This denotes the new month value of the date. This example sets the new value of the month of February as 1.

The output of this code is shown in Figure 9-17.

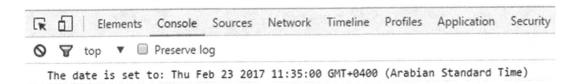

Figure 9-17. Program output

Summary

This chapter presented several of the basic objects you will encounter when working in JavaScript, including arrays, Booleans, strings, and dates. It described some of the properties and methods associated with them and showed you how to use them to write JS code.

In Chapter 10, you will explore the JSON format.

JavaScript Object Notation (JSON)

This chapter introduces the various ways you can use JavaScript Object Notation. It starts with an overview of JSON and then dives into the details of the data types used in JSON. You will then see how the JSON arrays and objects work in JS programs. Finally, you will see two useful methods, parse and stringify, of the JSON object.

JSON: An Overview

JSON is a form of data representation that lets you arrange interchangeable information in an organized manner. JSON is in text form (human-readable) and resides in a file. The usual file extension associated to JSON files is .json.

Note Apart from JavaScript, JSON may be used for Java, Python, Perl, etc. JSON may be used to exchange data between a browser and a server.

The syntax of JSON is a subset of JavaScript syntax consisting of data having name and value pairs.

The objects are contained in curly brackets, {}, separated by commas, whereas Objects and each name followed by colon (:). Arrays are contained within square brackets, [], and values are separated by commas.

```
var Employee = { "name":"Twinkle", "empid":1234, "position":"Trainer", "city":"London" }
var Company = { "Employee": [
                { "name":"Twinkle", "empid":1234, "position":"Trainer", "city":"London" },
                { "name":"John", "empid":4536, "position":"Associate", "city":"Denver" }
                ] }
```

Consider the example presented in Listing 10-1.

© Rehan Zaidi 2017

R. Zaidi, *JavaScript Essentials for SAP ABAP Developers*, DOI 10.1007/978-1-4842-2220-1_10

Listing 10-1. JSON Example

```
<html>
    <body>
        <script>
            var empObj;
            empObj = { "name":"Kelvin Desouza", "empId":17924, "designation":"Trainer",
            "city":"London" };
             console.log(empObj.name + " " + empObj.empId);
        </script>
    </body>
</html>
```

In this code, you can see the creation of an object with JavaScript using JSON-like syntax. This example declares the variable named empObj, assigns to it some name/value pairs, and then accesses the objects' values using dot notation. Only the employee name and ID are specified in the console.log method, so only those two values will be displayed in the web browser console.

The output of Listing 10-1 is shown in Figure 10-1.

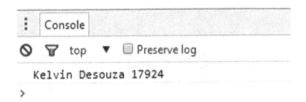

Figure 10-1. *Output*

JSON Data Types

JSON has the following data types:

- *Number*: Numbers in JSON cannot appear within quotes, and are usually integer or floating point. For example:

  ```
  { "empid": 123 }
  ```

- *String*: JSON strings are written in double quotes. For example:

  ```
  { "empname": "Twinkle" }
  ```

- *Boolean*: The value may be true or false. For example:

  ```
  { "Pass":true }
  ```

- *Object*: A JSON object can be any set of pairs of values. For example:

  ```
  {
  "Employee":  { "name":"Twinkle", "empid":1234, "position":"Trainer",
  "city":"London" }
  }
  ```

- *Array:* - the values can be grouped in an array. For example:

```
{
"Employee":  [ "name":"Twinkle", "empid":1234, "position":"Trainer",
"city":"London" ]
}
```

- *Null:* These are empty or no values. For example:

```
{ "value":null }
```

JSON Objects

The syntax of JSON objects is

```
var Employee = { "name":"Twinkle", "empid":1234, "position":"Trainer", "city":"London" }
```

As previously mentioned, the JSON objects are within curly brackets, {}, and contain key-value pairs that are separated by a colon (:). The key in the case of objects is also always a string that is within double quotes. The values pertaining to these keys may be of any data types (such as number, string, array, and so on).

There are two ways to access the object values: using dot (.) notation, like Employee.name, or by placing the value in brackets, like Employee["name"].

There are three ways to create JSON objects via JS coding:

- Create an empty object:

```
var myEm = {};
```

- Create a new object:

```
var myEm = new Object();
```

- Create a JSON object with key/value pairs:

```
var myEm = { "name":"Twinkle", "empid":1234, "position":"Trainer",
"city":"London" }
```

Listing 10-2 shows a fully working example.

Listing 10-2. JSON Object Example

```
<html>
   <body>
     <script>
         var product, val;
         product = { "prname":"Smart Phone", "price":20000, "company":"Sony",
         "camera":null };
         console.log( "Product name is: " + product["prname"] + " company: " +
         product["company"] );
     </script>
   </body>
</html>
```

This code is the same as code shown in Listing 10-1. This example accesses the values by using square brackets. In this case, the product name and company are accessed, so the required output will be the product name and company. The output of Listing 10-2 is shown in Figure 10-2.

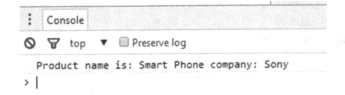

Figure 10-2. *Output*

JSON Arrays

The values are in the form of array as in JavaScript. The values are held in square brackets, [], and array values can be of any data types (number, string, array, object, Boolean, or null).

```
{
"soldin" : [ "US", "UK" ]
}
```

To access array values, use an index number like this:

```
soldin[1];
```

To better understand this concept, consider Listing 10-3.

Listing 10-3. JSON Array Example

```html
<html>
    <body>
        <script>
            var sellingitem;
            sellingitem = {
                        "itemname":"Smart Phone",
                        "itemprice":20000,
                        "soldin":[ "US","UK" ]
                        };
            console.log( "Product " + sellingitem.itemname +
                        " is sold in " + sellingitem.soldin[0] + ' and ' +
                        sellingitem.soldin[1] );
        </script>
    </body>
</html>
```

This example has a variable `sellingitem` that represents an object, with suitable values assigned to it. Within this object is an array `soldin` that contains the countries in which the item is sold. The `console.log` method is used to print the product name and the countries in the console. The output of Listing 10-3 is shown in Figure 10-3.

Figure 10-3. *Output*

In this case, we've defined a JSON array for a key value company with different attributes like Sony, Apple, Lenovo, and Samsung. Now, to access this array value, we use an index number with an object. So in this way we can identify a product brand name from a JSON array.

JSON parse Method

The parse method allows you to convert a data stream received in the form of a string (i.e., information in JSON form) into a JS object. To better understand the usage of the method, consider a scenario where you have a string containing name , ID , position, and trainer data pertaining to an employee. The parse method will use this as follows:

```
var Employee = JSON.parse('{ "name":"Twinkle", "empid":1234, "position":"Trainer",
"city":"London" }');
```

The parse method will take as input the entire JSON represented in string form. The result of this method execution will be returned in the form of an employee object.

The complete code for this example is shown in Listing 10-4.

Listing 10-4. JSON parse Method Example

```
<html>
    <body>
        <script>
            var Employee;
            Employee = JSON.parse('{ "name":"Twinkle", "empid":1234, "position":"Trainer",
            "city":"London" }');
            console.log( "Employee name:" + Employee.name + " Position:" + Employee.position );
        </script>
    </body>
</html>
```

This example declares the variable Employee and defines the text using JavaScript function JSON. parse(). The given text is converted to a JavaScript object. The output of Listing 10-4 is shown in Figure 10-4.

```
┌─────────────────────────────────────────────┐
│ ⋮  Console                                    │
├─────────────────────────────────────────────┤
│ ⊘  ▼  top    ▼  ☐ Preserve log               │
│                                               │
│   Employee name:Twinkle Position:Trainer      │
│ >                                             │
└─────────────────────────────────────────────┘
```

Figure 10-4. *Output*

JSON stringify Method

In contrast to the `parse` method, the `stringify` method does the reverse process. The method takes as input a JS object (as in the previous example, an Employee object) defined within a program.

```
var Employee = { "name":"Twinkle", "empid":1234, "position":"Trainer", "city":"London" };
```

This employee object will then be converted to a JSON string form.
Consider the example of the `stringify` method shown in Listing 10-5.

Listing 10-5. JSON stringify Method Example

```html
<html>
  <body>
    <script>
        var Employee, EmpStrg;
        Employee = { "name":"Twinkle", "empid":1234, "position":"Trainer",
        "city":"London" };
        EmpStrg = JSON.stringify(Employee);
        console.log( EmpStrg );
    </script>
  </body>
</html>
```

This example declares two variables, `Employee` and `EmpStrg`, and then defines the JavaScript object and assigns it to variable `Employee`. Next, using the JavaScript function `JSON.stringify()`, the given object is converted to string format. The output of Listing 10-5 is shown in Figure 10-5.

```
┌─────────────────────────────────────────────────────────────┐
│ ⋮  Console                                                    │
├─────────────────────────────────────────────────────────────┤
│ ⊘  ▼  top    ▼  ☐ Preserve log                               │
│                                                               │
│   {"name":"Twinkle","empid":1234,"position":"Trainer","city":"London"} │
│ >                                                             │
└─────────────────────────────────────────────────────────────┘
```

Figure 10-5. *Output*

Summary

This chapter introduced the basics of JSON and the data types that are used in JSON. It covered how the JSON arrays and objects work, and discussed the useful methods `parse` and `stringify` of the JSON object, along with code examples.

The next and final chapter presents best practices used in writing better JS coding, as well as some of the typical errors to avoid.

Summary

CHAPTER 11

■ ■ ■

Miscellaneous Topics

This chapter covers topics that are very useful but do not fit well in any of the earlier chapters. It starts with an overview of strict mode and how it affects the syntax check, as well as error handling in JavaScript. Next, you are provided tips related to code formatting and suggestions for using a naming convention for variables. A separate section explains debugging and troubleshooting JS programs. Last but not least, this chapter provides best practices for JS programming and offers some performance-improvement tips.

Strict Mode

Using strict mode enables developers to add stringent syntax checking to JavaScript code. For example, when strict mode is used, you cannot have a variable that is not declared explicitly, and you cannot use the with keyword. Most new versions of browsers implement strict mode.

The simplest way of activating strict mode is to add "use strict" at the start of a program or a function. The area within the program to which strict mode is applicable depends on where "use strict" is inserted. If you insert "use strict" outside a function (i.e., globally), the entire code of the program is checked for strict mode. On the other hand, if you insert it within a function's code, only the code within the function is checked using strict mode rules.

An example of code that uses strict mode is shown in Figure 11-1.

```
<html>
    <body>
        <script>
          "use strict";
          num = 10;  ⊗
          alert(num);
        </script>
    </body>
</html>
```

Figure 11-1. *Use of strict mode*

As you can see, the code attempts to define the variable num without using var declaration. Because strict mode is activated, the code gives an error as shown.

© Rehan Zaidi 2017
R. Zaidi, *JavaScript Essentials for SAP ABAP Developers*, DOI 10.1007/978-1-4842-2220-1_11

Now, consider the example of using strict mode in a function shown in Figure 11-2.

```
1  <html>
2    <body>
3      <script>
4      var myObj1 = { att1: 10, att2: 15, att1: 20 };
5      function my() {
6      "use strict";
7      var myObj = { att1: 10, att2: 15, att1: 20 };
8      }
9      }
10     </script>
11   </body>
12 </html>
13
```

Figure 11-2. *Use of strict mode in a function*

Here, strict mode is applied only to the function my(). Although both objects myObj and myObj1 contain duplication of the property att1, only one error is displayed, for the object within the function. No error results in the first object defined outside the function.

Usage of strict mode has the following advantages:

- It does not allow programming that might make code difficult to understand. Thus, it makes programs easier to understand and maintain.

- It helps to identify at an early stage of development errors that are not very safe to use or may give exceptions at the time of code execution.

Some of the constructs that are not allowed in strict mode are:

- *Repetition of a property*: Having multiple definitions of a property within an object literal is not permitted. Consider the following, which includes the property att1 twice:

  ```
  var myObj = { att1: 10, att2: 15, att1: 20 };
  alert(myObj.att1);
  ```

- This code without strict mode compiles and displays 20 in the browser alert box. If "use strict" is used, this code generates an error.

- *Duplicate function parameter*: Within strict mode, using a parameter name (formal) multiple times for a function is not allowed. Consider the following example:

  ```
  function myFunc(p1, p1){
      return p1;
  };

  alert(myFunc(10, 10));
  ```

Without strict mode, this code displays 10. However, when strict mode is used, the error shown in Figure 11-3 results.

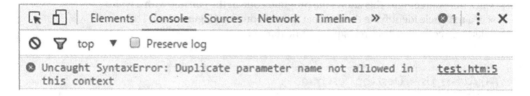

Figure 11-3. *Syntax error caused by duplicate parameter name*

- *Function declaration in code block*: When using strict mode, declaration of functions with a block of code is not allowed. Within strict mode, functions may only be defined at the topmost level of a program or within a function body. The following example is not allowed:

```
"use strict"
 for (var i = 0; i < 10; i++) {
     function myfunc() {
     }
 }
```

- *Use of the with statement*: Within strict mode, use of the with statement is not allowed.

Debugging JavaScript

As with all languages, JavaScript requires debugging. This section demonstrates how to debug a program in the Google Chrome browser in case you run the program and there are no errors directly displayed within the browser.

Consider the code:

```
<html>
    <body>
        <script>

            var num1 = 10;
            alert(num1) ;
            num =   1;
        </script>
    </body>
</html>
```

As you can see, num is not declared. However, when the code is executed within a browser, the alert box is still displayed (i.e., until the point at which the code is no longer correct).

To switch on and explore the debugger in the Chrome browser, follow these steps:

1. Press Ctrl+Shift+I. This opens the Console tab on the right side of the browser.

2. Click the Sources tab. This shows the program code in the console with a white × in a red circle identifying the line that is erroneous (see Figure 11-4). The offending code also has a red squiggly line under it.

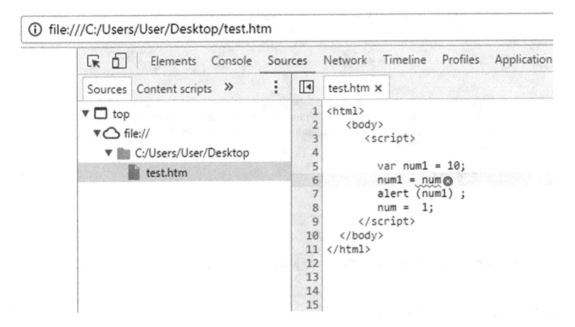

Figure 11-4. *Source code error*

3. Click the Console tab to see the text of the error, as shown in Figure 11-5.

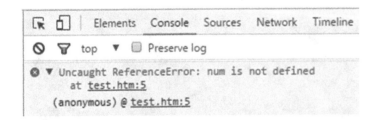

Figure 11-5. *Syntax error*

Suppose your program has no syntax errors but has certain logical errors, and you are not sure what exactly the cause is. In this case, you first need to find a suitable place to put a break point and then need to see the various statement executions as well as the content of the variables that are used.

To start the debugger, press Ctrl+Shift+I and then select the Sources tab. Click the line number where you want to put the breakpoint. Make sure that you click the line number, not the code itself. The breakpoint is displayed as a blue-highlighted arrow over the line number, as shown in Figure 11-6 on line 6.

Next, rerun the HTML page. This will rerun the JS code and the debugger will stop at the breakpoint; the left side of the screen will say "Debugger paused," as shown in the bottom-left pane of Figure 11-6.

To view the contents of a variable, in the lower-right pane of the screen, click the Watch tab. Click the + button. In the small pop-up text box, enter the name of the variable whose content you need to see—for purposes of this example, a1. This displays the value of a1 in the Watch area, as shown in Figure 11-6.

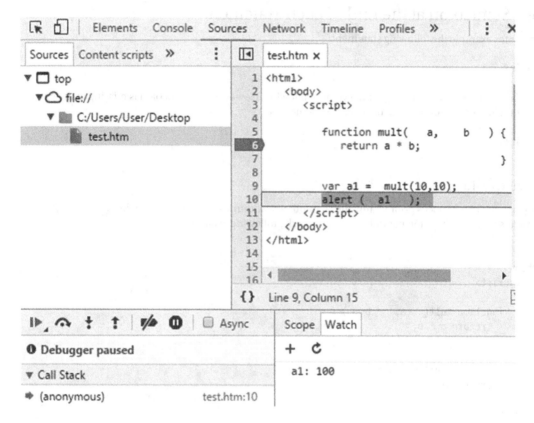

Figure 11-6. Breakpoint in browser console

You may use the following functions to proceed:

- To step over the next function call, press F10.

- To step into the next function call, press F11.

- To step out of the current function, press Shift+F11.

In order to exist the variable debugger, press F8. In order to deactivate all breakpoints, press CTRL+F8.

As you will see, once you proceed within the code, the line currently being executed will be highlighted in blue.

Code Formatting Tips

This section offers recommendations pertaining to your JS code formatting. These tips will make your code easier to understand and will not affect the syntactic check result.

Use a Semicolon at the End of Each Statement

Consider for example the following statement:

```
int = int + 1
```

This statement compiles nicely and gives the following. However, the semicolon is missing at the end of the statement. The recommended form of the statement is

```
int = int + 1;
```

Usage of Blanks

Do not use any blank spaces prior to and after parentheses within your code. These include any function parameters as well as function parameters. Consider the following example:

```
<html>
    <body>
        <script>

            function mult(    a,    b  ) {
                return a * b;
                                    }

            var a1 =  mult(    10,10);
            alert ( a1  );
        </script>
    </body>
</html>
```

Unnecessary blank spaces appear within the function `mult` before and after parameters a and b. Likewise, extra spaces appear while calling the function `mult`. Even the `alert` function call contains extraneous blank spaces. Such coding must be avoided. Here is the correct form of the previous example:

```
function mult(a,b) {
    return a * b;
}
var a1 =  mult(10,10);
alert (a1);
```

Always use blank spaces after `switch`, `while`, `for`, `if`, `else`, `try`, `catch`, and `finally`. In addition, always use blank spaces after curly brackets, next to operators, and even after wiring commas such as function parameters.

Usage of Comparison Operators

You should always use ! == and === in place of == and ! =, respectively.

Function Curly Brackets

Make sure that the opening curly bracket ({) for if, else, for, and switch statements and for function calls is on the same line as the statement keyword or function (whichever is applicable).

For example, consider the following:

```
function mult(a,b)
  {
   return a * b;
            }
```

The correct form is

```
function mult(a,b) {
   return a * b;
 }
```

Correctly Formatted Code Example

An example of correctly formatted code that incorporates all the preceding tips looks like this:

```
function myfunction(a1, a2) {
        var b2 = a1 / a2;
        if (b2 === 1) {
            b2--;
        }
        for (var a = 0; a < b2; a++) {
            alert(b2);
        }
        function func2(a1, b2) {
            return (b2 * a1) + b2;
        }

        return func2(2, 4);
    }
```

Naming Convention for Variables

I strongly recommend that you use a consistent naming convention for your JavaScript variables. The prefix of a variable must denote the type of the variable. I also recommend using the camelCase naming convention, with the prefix in lowercase and then continue with uppercase. I recommend using the example naming convention shown in Table 11-1.

Table 11-1. *Naming Convention Examples*

Type	Example
String	Name
Boolean	bFilled
Date	dYesterday
Object	oDomObj
Float	fWeight
RegExp	rSearchPattern
Function	fnDivide
Function parameters	mParameters
Array	aEntries

■ **Note**   You may be required to follow a naming convention based on company/project code standards that is different from what I have proposed here. The important thing is that you use a consistent set of naming conventions throughout your project.

Runtime Error and Exception Handling

Exceptions (also sometimes referred to as runtime errors) may happen during the execution of a program; that is, after compilation. For example, the following line results in an exception:

```
<html>
    <body>
        <script>

            abc("message");

        </script>
    </body>
</html>
```

In this case, the syntax is correct. However, at the time of execution, the code is trying to call a function that does not exist.

Exceptions may be caught via the try...catch...finally block. Using the block, you may catch both developer-generated exceptions and runtime exceptions. However, JS syntax errors may not be caught using this approach.

The syntax of a typical try...catch...finally block is shown here:

```
<script>

    try {
        //  code to be executed
    }
```

```
catch ( e ) {
  // Code to be executed when exception happens
  }

[ finally {
    // this part of code is run irrespective of whether an exception happens or not

  }]
```

```
</script>
```

When coding, the first block is the try block. After this, you may have one catch block or a finally block (or both). The finally block is optional. If an exception occurs within the try block, it is placed in error object e and the code within the catch block is run.

The catch block is supplied with the error object that contains relevant information about the error that has occurred. The error object has three properties:

- name: Error name
- message: Error message
- description: Description of the error

In addition, the error name may be one of several types; a few important ones are shown here:

- ReferenceError: Illegal reference
- TypeError: Type error
- RangeError: Number is not in range
- SyntaxError: Syntax error

After try/catch, any code within the finally block is run irrespective of whether an exception occurs or not.

Now that you have some knowledge of how exception handling occurs within the JS arena, you are ready to see some exception-handling code in action. Suppose you have the following block of code:

```
<html>
    <body>
      <script>
          abcd("This message");
      </script>
    </body>
</html>
```

As you can see, the program calls a nonexistent function by the name of abcd.

This block of code results in a runtime error. To change this program to catch the exception and display the description of the error in an alert box, you would use the following code:

```
<html>
    <body>
      <script>
          try {
            abcd("This message");
          }
```

```
        catch ( exception ) {
          alert("An exception occurred, the description of which is: " + exception.
          description );
        }

    </script>
  </body>
</html>
```

The code of the attempted abcd function call is placed within the try block. The alert box code is placed in the catch block. The exception object will contain necessary information about the error that occurred. This information will be displayed in an alert box.

The output of the program is shown in Figure 11-7.

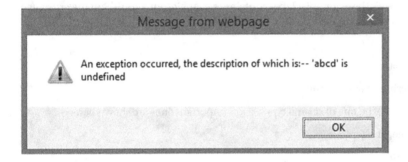

Figure 11-7. *Exception handled*

Best Practices in JavaScript

This section provides an overview of some of the best practices to implement in your use of the JavaScript language. These include tips and tricks such as avoiding the use of global variables and the use of closures, assigning default values to parameters, and always using a default clause in switch statements.

Avoid Use of Global Variables

It is recommended to avoid the use of global variables in JS. When you have a choice, use local variables. Never define data and objects as well as functions globally. As a default behavior, JS brings all declarations to the top. However, make sure to write data declarations at the top of the program at the time of coding.

Always keep data declarations at the top of the code. This includes keeping data at the top of the main program or any functions used. By following this practice, the code not only looks neat and clean, but also is easy to change because all the data declared is at the top. The following example shows this practice.

```
var myPlayerName, myWeight, myHeight;
myPlayerName = "James";
myWeight = 201.1;
myHeight = 85;
```

Even for loops, make sure that any variables used are declared at the top:

```
var a;
for (a = 0; a < 10; a++) {
}
```

Never Declare Objects for Numbers, Strings, or Booleans

Declaring objects for numbers, strings, or Booleans may have an adverse effect on the performance, and may not produce correct results.

Consider the following, in which the comparison returns `false`:

```
var myString1 = "James";
var myString2 = new String("James");
console.log((myString1===myString2));   // false
```

Now consider the following example:

```
var myString1 = new String("James");
var myString2 = new String("James");
console.log((myString1==myString2));    // false
console.log((myString1===myString2));   // false
```

Both the statements of comparison return `false`, because you cannot compare objects (in this case, string objects).

Use of default Clause in switch Statements

When using a `switch` control statement, always use a default clause. Consider the following example:

```
switch (num) {
    case 0:
        value = "Off";
        break;
    case 1:
        value = "On";
        break;
}
```

In this case, only two outcomes are possible; no `default` clause is included. Thus, when the value of num is neither 0 nor 1, you won't know what happened. I recommend using a `default` clause even if you think it will not be necessary.

The correct form of this example is

```
switch (num) {
    case 0:
        value = "Off";
        break;
```

```
    case 1:
        value = "On";
        break;
    default:
        value = "Unknown";
}
```

The default clause passes the value as Unknown when the value of num is neither 0 nor 1.

Assigning Default Values in Parameter

It is a good practice to assign default (initial) values to parameters within a function, corresponding to arguments that you anticipate may have undefined values.

Consider the following example:

```
function function1(a,b) {
..
}
```

In this case, if no value is passed for parameter b when calling function 1, the output is as follows:

```
  function1(10);
```

Because no value is passed for b, function1 may crash and/or result in an exception.

It is therefore recommended that you assign default/initial values to such arguments at the beginning of the function code:

```
function function1(a,b) {
    if (b === undefined) {
        b = 1;
    }
.....
}
```

Use === Comparison

It is recommended to use === instead of == when doing comparisons. The === operator performs both value and type comparison, whereas the == operator only performs value comparison (content check).

To better understand the difference, consider the following:

```
<html>
  <body>
    <script>
      console.log(8=="8");     // true
      console.log(8==="8");    // false
      console.log(0==false);   // true
      console.log(1==true);    // true
      console.log(0===false);  // false
      console.log(1===true);   // false
    </script>
  </body>
</html>
```

Here, the == and === operators are used to compare numbers with Boolean true and false. The output of the program is shown in Figure 11-8.

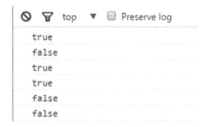

Figure 11-8. *Program output*

Avoid Usage of Closures

It is also recommended not to use closure, for performance reasons.

Consider the following:

```
Player.obj = function() {

    this.method1 = function() {

    };
}
```

Each time an instance of Player.obj is created, a function and corresponding closure get created for method1. Alternately, a better approach is

```
Player.obj = function() {

};

Player.obj.prototype.method1 = function() {

};
```

Using this approach, a single function is created for method1 without any closures, regardless of how many instances of Player.obj are created.

Summary

This final chapter pulled together the miscellaneous JS topics that will help you improve your programs. It started with an overview of strict mode and how it affects the syntax check. Next, you saw how error and exception handling is implemented in JavaScript. This was followed by an introduction to debugging and troubleshooting JS programs. The chapter wrapped up with best practices for JS programming as well as performance-improvement tips.

Index

Get the eBook for only $5!

Why limit yourself?

With most of our titles available in both PDF and ePUB format, you can access your content wherever and however you wish—on your PC, phone, tablet, or reader.

Since you've purchased this print book, we are happy to offer you the eBook for just $5.

To learn more, go to http://www.apress.com/companion or contact support@apress.com.

Apress®

Printed in the United States
By Bookmasters